MW00943613

Jailbreak

Cory Rice

Jailbreak
Copyright © 2016 Cory Rice
All rights reserved.

This book or parts thereof may not be reproduced in any form,
stored in a retrieval system, or transmitted in any form by any
means – electronic, mechanical, photocopy, recording, or otherwise
– without prior written permission of the publisher, except as
provided by United States of America copyright law.

All Scripture quotations, unless otherwise indicated, are taken from
the Holy Bible, New International Version®, NIV®. Copyright ©
1973, 1978, 1984, 2011 by Biblica, Inc.™ Used by permission of
Zondervan. All rights reserved worldwide.

Scripture quotations marked The Message are taken from *The
Message*. Copyright © 1993, 1994, 1995, 1996, 2000, 2001, 2002.
Used by permission of NavPress Publishing Group.

While the author has made every effort to provide accurate
Internet addresses at the time of publication, neither the publisher
nor the author assumes any responsibility for errors or for changes
that occur after publication.

Printed by CreateSpace, An Amazon.com Company

Visit www.hisandherjailbreak.com for more information.

ISBN: 978-1532907319

Cover design by Daniel Shouse (danielshouse.co)

THANK YOU

All financial proceeds from this book will go towards our own personal adoption story. Julia and I have a huge desire to adopt several children from different places around the world and you are helping this dream become a reality. My wife was adopted from Ukraine at age 16 and her life was drastically changed. We as a family want to do the same by changing the trajectory of the lives we are blessed with through adoption.

For more information visit: www.hisandherjailbreak.com

CONTENTS

INTRODUCTION

This book was written for myself! It is about my journey to sonship and a declaration of who my Daddy is. It is my hope that these pages make a real impact on your life. They will challenge the way you view God and how you view yourself, but I cannot take the credit. Over the last several years I have been greatly influenced by many men and women, and these words are a reflection of the influence they have made in my spiritual walk with God. This book is an overflow of the council, wisdom, and encouragement I have received throughout my journey to sonship.

As Eric Timm said of his book *Static Jedi*:

> "The purpose of a motivational book is to get you going. The end game of a self-help book is to get you to change. The prize of an inspirational book is to get you to feel better. **The goal of this book is worship**." [1]

CHAPTER 1

PROVE IT

If you're anything like me, you don't like many rules. I think that's why my parents were a bit shocked when I chose to go to Liberty University, a Christian college with rules...and a lot of them. The joke of our family quickly turned from me graduating in four years to making it through four weeks without getting kicked out. Luckily, the dean showed me grace in my first couple visits to his office that first month. The first time I met him was due to the stolen paper mâché hockey 'mascot' that was supposed to be the main float in the homecoming parade. To be clear, I didn't steal it. I mean, how can you steal a two-story tall homecoming parade attraction? I simply moved it with the help of some teammates. It was very comical to watch 20 guys move it back to its appropriate location several times throughout my first week. My meeting with the dean only happened because the last time we moved this mascot an RA caught us. And by us, I mean only me. That's what happens when you break into a building past curfew and pull a giant mascot onto the roof of a science department for all to see. Amazingly, I graduated six years later with two master's degrees. Some people would call it a miracle; others would say I proved my point.

Have you ever had one of those phrases you overuse or say so much it becomes annoying for others? One of those phrases for me is 'prove it'. We all have that one friend who tells the most ridiculous stories, most of which are hilarious but rarely ever true. There is nothing that rattles that guy more than telling him to 'prove it'. One of the funniest yet pointless arguments I have ever witnessed happened after hockey practice my senior year between our captain, Joe Smith, and his roommate, Brent Boschman. Brent claimed he could eat three boxes of macaroni and cheese in under thirty minutes. The next two words out of Joe's mouth were, 'prove it'; so he did. Twenty-three minutes later, Brent had devoured three whole boxes of macaroni and cheese all by himself.

The reality is, a lot of us are like Joe. We want to see evidence of the claims we hear because we're skeptics at heart. We tend to live in a state of disbelief because our worries, uncertainties, doubts, and life experiences cause us to want people to prove things. Such life circumstances form what we believe, and what we believe determines how we live. How we live often demonstrates whether we're walking with God or running from Him.

Most of us have faith or belief in something or someone. We have faith our car will get us from point A to point B. We have faith in our spouse and our friendships. We have faith in maps even though we have never been to space to really see if there are oceans separating countries and that the Earth is indeed round. We have faith our teachers are actually teaching us the right information. We have faith in our teammates. We have faith that they are working hard and that they too, want to win a National Championship. We hope they're not just in it for the free gear, the fame, and the girls. Whatever it is we believe, we have faith in it; and more faith than we even realize. Whether it's in a deity, science, or ourselves, our faith drives the way we treat people. It determines what we do when no one is looking and it is how we find happiness and pleasure during our lifetime.

If we don't have faith in God, we have put our faith in something or someone without even realizing it; or maybe we do realize it, and that's why we choose to trust science or believe God doesn't exist. Agnostics have asked me how I can put my faith in Jesus without physically seeing Him. Before I give my answer, I respond with a question of my own: 'How can you put your faith in the big bang theory without physically seeing it?' Have you ever noticed in Scripture how Jesus almost always answers a question with a question? Why do some Christians feel the need to argue or prove people wrong? Jesus didn't come to Earth to win arguments or prove His point. He came to make a difference. He came to love all people and set us free. The reality is, it takes as much faith to believe in Jesus as it does to believe in anything else. Christianity makes sense to me because I had my own experience with Jesus, an experience I would love all people to have.

I love to experience weird food combinations. I like ketchup on my eggs, peanut butter on my bananas, and french fries dipped in ice cream. I have a personal rule to never tell someone their food combination is gross without trying it first. You never know if you're missing out on a delicious food experience unless you try some things that seem weird or different. The same is true with Christianity. Psalm 34:8 says, "Taste and see that the Lord is good." In order to have an experience with something, we have to taste it! We have to taste the love and grace of God to recognize how amazing He is. We have to have our own encounter with this God who is crazy about us and who wants us to experience His love!

It was spring break my senior year of college when my friend Steve and I went down to Palm Beach, Florida. We ran into some friends there who convinced us to go surfing with them. Now I had never surfed before, so when Steve asked me if I wanted to wear a wetsuit my response was a simple: 'naw, I got this'. Huge mistake! Because I had never experienced surfing, I didn't know wetsuits were a must. I thought they were only to keep you warm, and because I am a northern boy, there is no ocean, lake, or river too cold for me to jump into. I passed on the wetsuit and paddled my way out to where all the surfer dudes were waiting on the perfect wave. After a couple hours of surfing, or eating waves in my case, we called it a day. I paddled in and started walking towards the shore when I see Steve laughing hysterically. That's when the pain from my chest hit me. I looked down and noticed that not only is my stomach completely chafed but my nipples were bleeding. That's right, I had bloody nipples. As Steve is laughing at me, he sarcastically says, 'You should have worn the wetsuit!' Noted...

I now know if I ever want to surf again, I must wear a wetsuit. I know because of an experience I had. So many people today refuse God before they even allow Him to show His incredible love. They walk away without ever experiencing His unconditional grace. They don't understand

4

that God is not mad, upset, or disappointed in us. Too many people believe they have out-sinned God's forgiveness and that there is no way a just God could give them a 'second chance'. However, the God of the Bible is not a God of second chances. He's the God of a second Adam. He's given us the amazing gift of His Son Jesus, the second Adam, who took our penalty, pain, and sin and completely destroyed them on the cross. This is why Christians use the phrase, 'born again'. We all have a natural birth (through Adam), but it's this second birth (through Christ, the second Adam) that gives people purpose on Earth. Jesus fulfilled every law so that we wouldn't have to and I believe God loves us and wants us to experience this amazing, never-ending, unconditional love.

Truth is, words on a page are not going to change us. The word of God doesn't even change us. Only application of the word of God changes us. It is possible to have been raised in a Christian home and still not live like Christ was raised from the grave. We can hear an incredible message about God from a pastor or read a great book and still take away nothing. We may even have a ton of Bible verses memorized yet lack an intimate relationship with Jesus. But when we experience God for who He really is, it changes everything. It changes the way we live and it even changes the way we interact with people.

You might be thinking, 'yeah that's great, just another pastor who's got it all together,' but you couldn't be further from the truth. My faith in Christ isn't always peaches and cream. My life is not perfect. Too often, people are sold on this false idea that Jesus makes life perfect, but when life throws a curveball and their dreams fall apart, so will their faith. Life with Christ doesn't mean we won't experience death, pain, and hurt. It does mean, however, that we can find joy even in those painful seasons because our perspective is different. Having a relationship with Jesus allows us to have peace, rest, and security in a God who never stops loving us even when we experience life's greatest challenges.

For me, my faith in Jesus wasn't always clear. I went through several seasons of doubt and unbelief. I've heard powerful sermons preached from Mark 9:23. It says, "Everything is possible for those who believe." The context of this whole passage is about Jesus healing a boy who was possessed by a demon. In the confusion and anxiety of this boy's father, the man asks Jesus to take pity on their family and heal his son *if He can*. Jesus responds to the man, *"If I can?"* I picture Him referencing Ezekiel 37 in this moment about the story where God the Father raises a valley of dry bones and puts together muscles, tendons, and flesh and breathes life into an army that used to be dead. *If I can...*

Again Mark 9:23 says, "Everything is possible for those who believe." I encourage you to trust Him even if your circumstances are difficult and don't make sense. But when pastors preach on this passage, they often leave out the next verse: Mark 9:24. Now, I can relate to Mark 9:24. The boy's father responds and says, "I do believe; help me overcome my unbelief!" What a pure and sincere plea! And if I'm being honest, I have been in that boat more often than I want to admit. I believe God to be Creator, Alpha and Omega. I believe in His power, but sometimes, I have moments of unbelief often triggered by moments of not understanding. I realize now that God is a big enough God to know and understand there will be moments in my life where I will doubt Him. I think God can handle my worries, fears, and uncertainties; so why am I so scared to be open about them?

I have to continually remind myself that the only way to overcome my unbelief is to be honest with God about it. God's not shocked, disappointed, or upset with us! He cares! 1 Peter 5:7 says, "Cast all your anxiety on Him because He cares for you!" He knows I'm struggling and He wants to reveal Himself to me, but He wants me to ask. Am I bold enough to admit where I have doubts and allow a loving God to prove how much He values me? I think this honest prayer from the boy's father is something I can learn from. God, I believe, help me overcome the unbelief in areas of my life.

Even now as a pastor, I have moments of doubt, but it's what I do with doubt that is important. When doubt creeps in, I have two options. I can either allow it to rip apart everything I believe and cause my faith to be stagnant with God, walking away from the only One who will never stop loving me; or I can seek after truth, allowing God to prove Himself faithful. This happened to me three months before I graduated college.

From an early age, especially as an athlete, I had big dreams of making it in professional hockey. I grew up in a hockey family where our second home was the ice rink. My mother was a phenomenal figure skater who coached on ice even while 9 months pregnant with my oldest brother. She would come into practices as our power skating coach and work us like rented mules. Our team hated those days and we were relieved at the end of practice as we sat in the locker room, bent over in a puddle of sweat, panting for air. Everyone would talk bad about her except me, because I had to go home with her!

My father, who was born and raised in Canada, played top tier junior hockey during his teenage years. He was good enough to be highly recruited by several universities who coveted his scoring ability. He landed at Michigan State in 1972 and, in three and a half years, he put up so many points that he's still the 5th all time leading scorer in MSU hockey history. He was dominant! I found an article written about him in 2008 from Wisconsin University's play-by-play broadcaster Paul Braun. He said the best power-play unit in college hockey history was a line in the 70's made up of Tom Ross, Steve Colp, John Sturges, and Daryl Rice. Combined, they put up more than 200 power-play goals and, when asked who the 5th member of the power-play unit was, Paul responded, "It didn't matter, you could put the equipment manager out with them and they were still going to score...even though it's nearly 40 years ago, I can still rattle off those names when I think of college hockey greats."[1] My dad was a stud! He went to professional camps with the Boston Bruins and Detroit Red Wings, played in the minors, and spent some time in Italy before hanging up the skates to marry the woman my travel teams loved to hate. The point is, hockey was our life. I had no bigger dream than making the pros and carrying on the legacy of my father. When I was able to play hockey at Liberty University, I believed this was the beginning of my road to glory.

I was sitting in the Vines Center on Liberty's Campus on a September night in 2006, when I heard a message from Clayton King. I felt God was leading me to consider student ministry and finally let go of my pro hockey dream. Over the next six months, I changed majors and started an internship with the student ministry at Oak Pointe Church in Michigan. At the end of the summer in 2007, I was convinced that pouring into students was what God wanted me to do and I fell in love with this age group. As a punk and practical joker myself, I fit right in. Even now, I sometimes need a reminder that I am, in fact, the leader. I will always talk about Jesus; it just might happen after I throw you into a bush. It's called a 'bush-push'. Spend an afternoon with me and I'll show you what I mean. I ended up interning at Oak Pointe Church over the next four summers and was really excited to eventually lead a student ministry of my own. I rode this 'spiritual high' for a while until reality approached and doubt started to creep in and manifest in my mind.

Fast forward to February 2009, three months before I graduated, when I began what turned into a 10-month struggle. I started doubting everything I believed. I was confused, didn't know where to turn, and constantly felt alone. You would have never known it if you knew me because I played it off so well. I started grappling with all kinds of questions about my faith. Questions like, is Christianity really true and how can I be for certain? What do the other religions believe and why are they all convinced they are right? I got angry with God and yelled at Him, "If you want me to devote my entire life to pouring into teenagers, then I need proof. I need to know 100% you are real!"

I'm convinced it's not the doubt that's bad. We all have doubts; even the disciples had doubts. Jesus said, *'You of little faith'* four times in the book of Matthew and three of those times were to his own disciples. That phrase literally means to not understand or describes someone as disinterested in walking intimately with God. The disciples didn't really understand who Jesus was yet. John 2:22 tells us the disciples didn't believe Jesus was the Messiah until after the resurrection. They didn't have the Bible to tell them what was going to happen in the end. It's easy for me to make fun of them because I have a cheat sheet (the Bible) but the reality is

9

they didn't know! They had their doubts. Peter gets out of the boat in Matthew 14. He takes his eyes off Jesus and, the moment he takes his eyes off Jesus, he sinks. The same is true for me. The moment I stop seeking Jesus is the moment I sink. Peter got back into the boat, rung out his clothes, and continued seeking after Christ. Remember, it was Peter who stood up boldly in Acts to preach and 3,000 people got saved.

Then, there's this disciple named Thomas. He gets a bad rep because he doubted the other disciples about Jesus' resurrection. Granted, he was the only disciple at the time not to see the resurrected Christ. All the other disciples had the privilege of seeing Jesus again and were telling Thomas about the experience. He said yeah right, 'prove it'. I mean, come on, that's a logical response. Jesus was dead! The dude helped with the burial process! Thomas wanted his own experience of seeing Jesus for himself and I resonate with Thomas a lot! He's known as 'doubting Thomas', but I would love to change that perspective. He didn't run from Christ or run from truth. Jesus appears to him, Thomas says 'prove it', and Jesus shows him His scars. Jesus reveals Himself to Thomas and gives him the proof he wanted. It's the disciple, Thomas, who then goes boldly sharing the good news of Jesus Christ and takes the Gospel farther east than any other disciple. He traveled outside the Roman Empire, all the way to India! Did you know it was this experience with Jesus that led him to give his life for the furthering of the Gospel? We so quickly forget it was Thomas in John 11:16 who said to the disciples, "Let us also go, that we may die with him." Thomas was all in! He made a huge impact and it started by seeking Christ through his doubts.

It's my belief that doubts have the ability to move us into a closer relationship with God as we seek Him through all areas of our lives. The most important thing, when it comes to doubt, is what we do with it. Many people have doubts about God so they give up hope. I've heard people say they don't believe anymore because of life's circumstances, or they believe the lie that God has given up on them so they give up on God. It doesn't matter how lonely we feel, God has been and will always be with us, whether we believe in Him or not. I believe doubt can be used as a great tool to teach us what it is we believe. Psalm 9:10 says, "Those who know your name will trust in you for you God have never forsaken those who seek you." There is beauty in that truth. If you are struggling with doubt, seek Him! Asking God to prove Himself is a great place to start.

CHAPTER 2

STAUROS

I was driving down highway 501 in Lynchburg right after practice, when I got angry with God and asked Him to prove He was the only way. I had so many unanswered questions and didn't know what I really believed. I was three months from graduating and about to devote my entire life to preaching His truth, but I didn't even know if it was true. It's comforting to know that even if I decided to walk away from God that day, God had no interest in ever walking away from me. I stopped by Kroger to pick up some groceries when I ran into someone from the seminary who knew me. He was a hockey fan decked out in a Liberty Hockey hoodie and went on to talk about how he had never been to a hockey game until this year. He became an instant fan! You get that a lot when you play a northern sport in a southern state. The fans love that you can check people into the boards and throw a couple punches, and it's all just 'a part of the game'. It threw me off that first game when the crowd cheered louder over a scrum after the whistle than they did when we scored a goal. Most southerners know very little about hockey. This guy knew I was a religion major and told me about how some of my undergrad credits could transfer into graduate school. I went home and immediately looked into it. I researched all the possible master's degrees and how long each took. To make a long story short, I didn't go to seminary to learn more about Scripture or to validate my calling or purpose in the Kingdom of God. I went in as a total skeptic. I was seeking after this 'truth' thing. I wasn't giving up on what I felt God call me into three years earlier. Rather, I was seeking whether or not Christianity was the real deal.

My first semester of graduate school was filled with Apologetics classes. I spent the first six months studying every major religion I could. I wanted to know what they really believed and I just happened to get class credit for it at the same time. I was fascinated by what I found. The God of the Bible was slowly showing me the reality behind these counterfeit gods and what each religion actually teaches and practices. God was revealing Himself to me through my own experience. I was about to taste and see the Lord is not only real, but He is good.

ISLAM

I spent most of my time first semester digesting Islam. Islam was established in 622 A.D. and stresses the submission to Allah, the Arabic name for God. It also claims truth like Christianity. In Islam, one has to conform to the five pillars of faith. They are disciplines that are essential for salvation. These five pillars of faith or disciplines are:

1. Shahada (The Confession of Faith) – one must confess that there is no god but Allah and that Muhammad is his prophet. If one later denies this confession, it nullifies the hope for salvation.

2. Salat (Prayer) – one must pray five times a day, properly wash beforehand, and pray facing Mecca. These five times of prayer occur before sunrise, noon, midafternoon, sunset, and prior to going to bed.

3. Zakat (Giving) – one must give two and one-half percent of all of their wealth to the poor. This is taught in the Qur'an, the Islamic holy book. This giving secures and purifies the remaining wealth of the giver.

4. Sawm (The Fast) – one must fast from sunrise to sunset for the entire lunar month of Ramadan. This includes withholding from sexual relations.

5. Hajj (The Pilgrimage) – one must make the journey to Mecca at least once in their lifetime. Once there, they must also participate in the mandatory walk seven times around the Kaabah (The Shrine of the Black Rock), which is the holiest place of Islam.

Muslims believe that Allah is unknowable personally, but that his will is revealed in the Qur'an and must be followed completely. The hope each Muslim has in salvation is that they did enough to obey the five pillars of faith as well as satisfy the will of Allah. Even the most obedient Muslims still fear judgment day as they continue to strive through their own efforts for the approval of their god.

In my experience, Muslims are very friendly. In fact, I hate to admit it but they are friendlier than most Christians I know. As I interact with them, it breaks my heart to find such dedicated people truly worshipping what they believe without real peace, rest, and security. They are constantly trying to do enough good works and be good people to please a god they have no relational interaction with. Salvation comes down to their own ability to gain the attention of Allah. The Muslims I encounter never really know if their good deeds successfully earn them a place in paradise. That thought alone is a fearful and anxious place to be.[1]

BUDDHISM

Buddhism was next on my list and turned out to be extremely interesting. Buddhism is all about finding enlightenment or true inner peace, but what I didn't know, is there is no personal relationship with the Buddha. It is actually an impersonal religion of perfecting yourself. In fact, its founder, Siddhartha Gautama, established Buddhism as a form of atheism because he rejected the idea of a personal God. He struggled with the reality of suffering, judgment, and evil. Therefore, he had difficulty believing in the existence of a good and just God.

The Buddhist belief systems are found in the Four Noble Truths and the Noble Eightfold Path. The Four Noble Truths are:

1. Dukkha – life is full of suffering.
2. Samudaya – suffering is caused by craving.
3. Nirodha – suffering will cease only when craving ceases.
4. The first three truths can be achieved by following the Noble Eightfold Path. The Noble Eightfold Path consists of having right views, right aspiration, right speech, right conduct, right livelihood, right effort, right mindfulness, and right contemplation.

Buddhists also believe in several key doctrines such as…

- Anicca – the belief that nothing in life is permanent.

- Anatta – the belief that they do not truly exist.
- Karma – the belief of cause and effect. If you do something bad, bad things will happen to you; if you do something good, good things will happen to you.
- Reincarnation – the belief in an endless cycle of continuous suffering, only broken by entering a permanent state of pure nonexistence, also known as nirvana.

The thing I found most interesting about Buddhism is that its followers are very concerned with suffering and overcoming it, yet they must deny suffering is even real. Their earthly struggle is about doing enough good deeds and rooting out their desires to break the cycle of suffering. They also have to convince themselves they have no personal significance, even though they live as if they do. All of this is done with the hope of finding inner peace (which they never will on Earth) and escaping the reality of life into a state of nirvana. This hope is really no hope at all, because with nirvana comes death and complete extinction, escaping the path of reincarnation. Buddhists struggle to make sense of the life they live because desire is never eliminated.[2]

HINDUISM

After Buddhism, I spent some time diving into Hinduism. Interestingly, as I am writing this, I recently had a conversation with a former Hindu named Rekha on the beautiful beaches of Aruba. Having studied Hinduism, I was able to speak directly into her current situation. After an hour of talking, I shared Jesus with her and talked with her about His amazing grace, love, and acceptance. I would love to tell you she gave her life to Christ, but that didn't happen. At the end of the conversation I told her these exact words, "Rekha, I know you don't believe in Jesus but if He was standing here with us right now He would want you to know He's proud of you and He loves you." Tears started flowing, she thanked me, hugged me, and turned and went on her way. I never saw her again, but my prayer is that God would continue to reveal Himself to her. Looking back on life, I believe the reason I specifically studied Hinduism in graduate school is because God knew I would be on a beach in Aruba four years later, sitting next to a woman who desperately needed to be told that God loved her. Hindus never hear that.

Hinduism has a pagan background and recognizes no final truth. The Hindu god is known as Brahman but is impersonal and unknowable. They also worship a multitude of other gods and goddesses through prayer, fasting, dance, and offerings. Most of the gods and goddesses of Hinduism have to do with forces of nature and personified human heroes. Hindus claim there are 330 million gods, and they can also choose whom it is they want to worship.

When it comes to creation, Hindus believe everything is actually an illusion. There is no beginning or end to creation, only endless cycles of life and destruction or reincarnation. Since everything is an illusion, history has little value, because history doesn't really exist. Because of this idea of living illusions, there is no such thing as rebellion against a Holy God. Humanity's problems are summed up as ignorance, desire, and violation of one's social duty. There is also no real concept of salvation. Life is all about self-realization. The only hope they have is to eventually get off the cycle of reincarnation. This occurs randomly, and when the illusion of your own personal existence dies, only then will you eventually become one with the impersonal god.[3]

18

It doesn't matter where you look, Christianity is the only religion in the world founded and based on love. It is the only religion where God comes to man. It is the only religion where God Himself paid the penalty for everyone, even for those who deny Him, through the life, death, and resurrection of Jesus. It is the only religion where God both makes and meets the demands. It is the only religion motivated by acceptance and grace. It is the only religion that has nothing to do with earning our own salvation. It is the only religion offering true peace, rest, and security. It is the only religion where God loves us even when we mess up. It is the only religion that offers hope, even in the midst of pain. It is the only religion where God is personal, knowable, and actively involved in our daily lives. Christianity does not use works, fear, manipulation, shame, or condemnation to motivate us into a real relationship with Christ, although some pastors wrongly do. It is the only religion where I don't have to gain the attention of God because I already have it; He knew me before I was in my mother's womb (Jeremiah 1:5, Psalm 139:13). It is the only religion where you don't have to 'get right', 'do more', or 'gain approval' because in Christ, He has already approved you! Christianity involves a relationship with the Creator. Through this experience, I not only learned what it is I truly believe, but also Whom I believe in. I believe in a God who is so passionate about me, He sent His only Son to die in my place. I believe in a God Whose love is so strong it never changes! I couldn't get over this radical and insane grace - a grace revealed to me through my doubts - a grace that changes everything.

I went into this season of my life with a ton of doubts. For months, I struggled with what I believed. However, instead of staying stagnant or running from my faith, I asked God to prove Himself. My doubts started with the question about other religions. So I researched them, and through that experience, God revealed Himself to me in a way I could have never imagined.

As I learned about Islam and interacted with Muslims, I couldn't get over the cross and everything it represents. Every time I studied, the cross grew bigger and bigger. The true Gospel message is not about our own works and efforts. It's not about getting the attention of God. It's not about rules, rituals, or regulations. It's not about fear or satisfying a need. It's not even about what I can offer God. The entirety of the Gospel is summed up completely in what Jesus did on the cross: His finished work on the cross. Jesus did everything I couldn't and more. He lived the perfect life. He fulfilled every prophecy and every law. He conquered sin and death. He died so we wouldn't have to, and He rose from the dead to share with us His goodness. Jesus did all the work! There is nothing for us to do to earn salvation or gain acceptance. Whether you believe in God or not, He already loves you, accepts you, and approves of you. The only 'work' you have to do is believe God to be who He says He is. There and only there will you find true peace, rest, and security.

In Buddhism there is no hope. There is no actual dealing with the suffering in our lives. There is no peace, and life becomes a hopeless cycle. Just because you don't like evil or can't really explain it doesn't mean you can stop it. Claiming that there is no God because there is evil does not fix the problem and reality of evil. The fact that there is evil in this world is actually proof to me that God does exist. Without evil, how do we know what good is? Without hate, how do we know what love is? Can we really understand the depth of love if we have not understood and experienced hate and suffering? To the Buddhist, real issues get swept under the rug, and the reason bad things happen is because of a belief in Karma.

Belief in Karma is actually a scapegoat and provides an opportunity to fake relationships, love, and 'good deeds'. If people only do good things to gain something in return, what does that tell you about them and their belief system? (Unfortunately, there are many Christians who have this kind of relationship with Jesus. The entitlement attitude exposes the real motives of the heart). Under Karma there is no mercy, no grace, no appeal, and no escape. It is all about perfecting yourself. Life in Buddhism becomes oppressive and helpless. What Buddhists don't understand is that desires aren't bad and aren't supposed to be eliminated. God has given us desires and pleasures on Earth to enjoy. The problem lies when we take those desires and pleasures out of context and seek them to satisfy our needs instead of being satisfied in Christ alone. This is why Buddhists constantly try to fight desire, because they have never experienced true fulfillment in Christ. When we live for ourselves, whether we are trying to perfect ourselves or not, desire only breeds suffering. This kind of suffering never stops and never allows you to enjoy life. Your only hope becomes the cycle of reincarnation. When you live in this state, without hope, peace, and nowhere to turn, the only hope you have is becoming extinct (or reaching nirvana). This hope in nirvana is no hope at all!

Speaking of hope, in Hinduism there is none. In fact, this religion doesn't make any sense to me. To believe that we are all illusions doesn't resonate with our souls. We are here for a purpose! A much larger purpose than just living for ourselves and believing we have little to no significance. You are important and you matter to Jesus. You matter so much that even in your sin, Christ died for you.

In Christianity, our hope comes in the form of what Jesus did for us. Thank God, because putting hope in yourself and your own efforts only breeds constant failure! If it was up to me to earn salvation, I would never achieve it, and neither would you. This is what makes Christ so amazing and so appealing. This is why it is so hard for some people to understand, because our human nature wants us to believe that we must do something to earn our salvation. But Christianity is the opposite. Salvation is ours if we only believe.

It was in the second semester of graduate school when all my doubts regarding Christianity had ceased. After studying all these religions and God revealing Himself to me, Christianity just made sense. Through every religion I studied, my mind just couldn't get over the cross. I mean, that Christ would die for me? I couldn't stop thinking about it. I was sitting in my mandatory Greek class one afternoon wanting to jump in front of a bus when Jesus became so incredibly real to me. We had been studying specific Greek words (the only part of Greek I enjoyed), when we landed that afternoon on the Greek word Stauros.

Stauros is the Greek word for cross. However, it carries so much more weight than that. Greek is a dead language and words can have multiple meanings, which is why there are so many different English translations of the Bible. But this one word, Stauros, gave the cross a different meaning for me. In this Jewish culture 2,000 years ago, the word Stauros carried such a weight that people would refrain from using it. When it was said, people would stop what they were doing. It had shock value! The Stauros was a form of death that was humiliating. This kind of death was actually invented by the Persians. Anyone that would not bow to the king would be brought in before him. The Persian soldiers would then make these prisoners turn around, so they couldn't look them in the face, as they stabbed them in the back with a spear. The soldiers would then lift the spear with the body dangling on it and stick it into the ground. Then they would watch as the breathing man would slowly slide down the spear, allowing his lungs to fill up with blood, as he would painfully suffocate to his death. Although the Persians invented the Stauros, it was the Romans who perfected it. They figured if you nail someone to the Stauros and stand them upright, you could do it in front of a crowd, it would last longer, and it would be more painful. The Romans used death by Stauros as a public display to warn people to not believe what this person believed and to not behave like they behaved.

To die a death of Stauros brought so much disgrace to a family that fathers would disown their own sons. It was an incredibly embarrassing way to die. In this culture, nudity literally was a form of shame, which is why no one would dare to be caught about in public nude. This is also why the Romans crucified people naked. It was the ultimate form of shame. Was Jesus naked on the cross? The Bible is not clear about that, but after studying this culture, I personally believe He was.

Not only was the Stauros a humiliating way to die, it was also extremely painful. When Stauros was used, not only would people think about death, they would also think about everything that led up to the death. Stauros meant the vote that allowed the guilty thug Barabbas to walk free. It meant the mocking, the punching, the beating, and the spitting. It meant His beard being ripped out of His face. It meant the crown of thorns being pushed down into His skull, which weren't your little thorns from the berry bush in your backyard. These were monstrous size thorns that were one to two inches long. It meant the blows to His body with clubs. It meant the lashes to His back from a leather whip (think Indiana Jones), and at the end of the whip were several leather strings. Attached to each leather string were sharp rocks, broken pieces of glass, and hooks, so every time Jesus was whipped, one of those rocks, glass shards, or hooks would attach to his flesh, muscles, and tendons and rip them apart. So when Jesus was then told to carry His cross up Calvary, He couldn't physically do it. It wasn't just because He was tired and beaten; it was because He literally didn't have the muscles in His back to lift it up. It meant the nails piercing His wrists and ankles. It meant the dangling in pain for three hours as He slowly died. The crazy thing about dying on the Stauros, was you died from suffocation. So, every time Jesus wanted to breathe, He would have to pull Himself up on the flesh that was nailed to the cross just to grasp some air. This is why the process on the cross took so painfully long.

In this culture, the 'poor people' also figured out how to make some extra change on the side. In Jerusalem, people would have to do their bathroom business outside the city walls in holes since they didn't have the luxury of indoor plumbing. The poor community figured they could make tips by wiping the feces from people as they finished doing their business. They fixed together sticks with sponges attached to them at the top. However, this was one of the reasons why disease spread so rapidly at this time, so they mixed together wine and vinegar to help sanitize their sponges. So when the soldier grabbed a stick with a sponge attached to it, dipped it in wine and vinegar and held it to the lips of Jesus, some scholars believe this sponge would have been used to wipe the feces off of humans, the same humans Jesus was dying for.

Everything we know about the crucifixion of Jesus was summed up with one Greek word. This is why Stauros carried so much weight. That word described the burden that Jesus carried. This is why it had shock value. Anytime anyone would hear this word, all those images of the cross would flash through their mind like a nightmare. Stauros became one of the most impactful words in my vocabulary. It is so simple for us Americans to talk about the cross with such ease, but when you get a revelation of the Stauros, it changes the game.

The understanding of what Stauros really meant brought so much clarity to what Jesus actually did for me. I am so thankful Jesus would endure all of that just for me, just for you. Jesus didn't die so we could be sorry; He died so we could experience His love. He went through the greatest pain to give us the greatest opportunity. Religions around the world all focus on our own efforts and good deeds for salvation. Christianity relies on believing in the finished work of Jesus on the Stauros. Religion says do more and be better, Jesus says *come to me and I will give you rest*!

In all of my doubts, God brought me to a place that revealed His love and grace I just couldn't ignore. A place of true peace in knowing God has a plan specifically for my life; a place of true rest in knowing that Jesus has paid the price in full; a place of true security in knowing that I am a son of the living King.

CHAPTER 3

WHO'S YOUR DADDY?

Did you notice that last sentence in the previous chapter? I'll say it again; God brings us to a place of true security in knowing He calls us sons and daughters. If we know Jesus as our Savior, we're His children. Galatians 3:26 says, "So in Christ Jesus you are all children of God through faith." 1 John 3:1 says, "See what great love the Father has lavished on us, that we should be called children of God! And that is what we are!" You are a daughter of Jehovah God; you are a son of the living Creator of the Universe. Think about that for a moment.

My pastor recently preached on the story of Walt Disney and his daughter, Diane, to help us better understand who our Daddy is. What a lot of people don't know about Walt Disney, according to his daughter Diane, is that he was just a 'normal dad'. She said that she didn't even discover who her dad was until the first day of kindergarten...

"'I sat in the middle of the room,' Diane recalled, 'and all of the students were introducing themselves. They got to me and I said, 'Well my name is Diane Disney.' The whole class went crazy! I almost started to cry and asked the teacher, 'Is something wrong?' The teacher said, 'No, everybody is just excited! Honey, say your name again?' 'My name is Diane Disney!' The whole class went crazy again! The teacher looked at me and said, 'Honey, I think I can tell you why the students are all excited. What is your dad's name?' 'My dad's name is Walter!' The class went crazy again! The teacher pulled me aside and said, 'Let me tell you why everybody is excited! Your dad is Walt Disney!' I said, 'Yeah, Walter Disney!' The teacher responded, 'No, your dad is Walt Disney…Disneyland! Mickey Mouse Club! Disney! That's your dad!' I went home that day; my dad was sitting in a chair reading the newspaper. I walked up to him, tore the newspaper out of his hand, put my little hands on my little hips, stared right at him and said, 'You never told me you were Walt Disney!' For months, I walked around stunned by who my father was!"[1]

I wonder how many believers do not realize who their Father is? Sonship is something that a lot of American Christians miss. When I talk about security in Christ, usually the first thing I'm asked is, "So you believe in eternal security?" Or they ask the question, "What do you believe about once saved, always saved?" Almost always I'll smile politely. I think it's comical how often we find ourselves speaking Christianese. We like to use big words and speak in theological sentences as if to impress others with how much we know. But what if we are asking the wrong questions? What do people really mean by 'eternal security'? I like to learn a lot about something by studying its antonym. The antonym for security would be insecurity. Grasp this for a minute. If Christ is my portion, provider, healer, comforter, security, etc, then I have nothing to be insecure about if my identity is truly found in Him. The problem here is a lot of people don't realize that when we believe in Jesus, He actually lives IN us! Do we recognize the same power that raised Jesus from the dead actually lives inside of us? Yet, this power is only released as we believe God to be who He says He is. So yes, I am eternally secure in knowing Christ's identity is now my identity. If Jesus is secure and He lives IN me, I'm eternally secure! In Jesus, there is no such thing as insecurity and this revelation started with understanding my sonship in Christ.

We throw out these Christianese expressions like 'once saved, always saved.' We hold on to this phrase when our loved ones walk away from Christ. We even argue about the eternal destinations of people who claim Christ yet turn to follow the world. Our response is often trying to defend if this person really had an experience with God or were they just punching their religious clock. Many people believe if we just attend church services, if we give our finances, if we serve in the community, or if we read the Bible it makes us all good with Jesus. We tend to find our identity in what 'we do' in Christianity instead of finding our identity in what 'Christ has done'. Bishop Jamie Englehart, a spiritual father of our church, recently challenged us by saying we should change this 'once saved, always saved' phrase to, 'once a son, always a son'. Once we know our identity in Christ, that we are a son or daughter of God, it changes the way we do life. It even changes the way we view church. We actually reflect what church should be when we think less about whether or not we can attend and more about who we want to bring.

One problem with churches today is there are far too many pastors who don't realize they are sons or daughters. We have too many spiritual orphans preaching rules and regulations, laws and principles. It is impossible to lead other people into sonship or daughterhood when we ourselves don't know who our Daddy is!

We struggle with identity more than we realize. When we don't know who we are and more importantly, whose we are, we end up living for and chasing after things that never satisfy. In today's world, we have let society shape the way we view ourselves, how we find our identity, our worth, and our importance.

Have you ever noticed how technology has taken over the world today? I work with all kinds of students and social media is bigger today than it has ever been. Who knows if it will even be relevant in the next several years. I often times find it humorous when my students don't know what a cassette tape is. They will never know what it is like to sit with your boom box listening to the radio for hours just waiting for 'your' jam to play again, just so you could press record on the tape deck. It would always drive me nuts when the disc jockey would talk through the last 15 seconds of the song. Then I'd have to wait for them to play the song again just to rerecord it. Students today don't even know what it's like to buy a whole CD just to find out the single was the only good song on the album. Today, they have iTunes to pick and choose what it is they want to buy. They will also never understand the phrase 'Be kind, please rewind'. I mean, even our middle school students have cell phones today with access to more information than they'll ever need. And don't even get me started on how technology works. It is beyond me! I have no idea how I can dial a number and talk with someone across the world. I don't understand how I can write something out on my phone and it appears as a text message to someone else. You can try to explain to me all you want, it just doesn't make sense. My brain does not comprehend how technology works.

Social media is what everyone is hooked on right now. It is not a bad thing. I can connect with people I would never be able to connect with. I can see what celebrities are doing and I have access to anyone's personal life at any time. However, there is no such thing as privacy in today's world because we like to share our lives with all of our 'followers'. No one cares about what you are eating and we have all seen the 47 pictures of your newborn baby. Also, please stop with the photo-shopped selfies. If you go missing, no one will know what you actually look like.

It's crazy how often I find myself constantly checking my news feed and creeping on people I don't even care about. Don't judge me, you do it too. Isn't it funny (or sad) how often we ignore real life people right in front of us to creep on people we don't even know? Then we get jealous because our life doesn't seem as great as what other people are sharing through social media.

As I think about the phenomenon of social media and what it has done for this next generation, I find it interesting how every single person in the world strives for acceptance. This is how our young people today feel valued. They care about how many people follow them on Twitter and

Instagram and they check all the time. I bet if you have Twitter or Instagram, you could tell me how many followers you have without having to look. They care about who is following them and who is not following them. They even have a website they log into to see who is not following them back and to see who recently unfollowed them. Then there is always that awkward conversation if you choose to confront this person on why they unfollowed you. It's probably because they don't care about the song lyrics you post every 14 minutes or your constant Twitter ramblings about #oomf (one of my friends/followers). They are aware of who retweeted and favorited their tweets. They check to make sure all of their friends liked their photo on Instagram and they constantly compare. If someone gets more retweets or more likes on a photo they get frustrated and jealous. Then, the next photo they release usually shows a little more skin, all in an effort to gain acceptance and value from their peers. According to a recent blog on the statistics of Instagram, "Our young people are given a numerical value on which to base his or her social standing. For the first time ever, our students can determine their 'worth' using actual numbers provided by their peers."[2] The reality is, they are paying attention. The problem is we don't know our importance, value, and worth. We don't see ourselves as God sees us. We don't know who our Daddy is.

You may be shocked to think your children are dealing with this but the truth is, it's the same with adults and parents. Maybe you have Facebook to brag about your kid's success because secretly that is where you find your value or worth as a parent. Maybe for you it's not social media at all. For you, it's running after a job or you think if you have that title or position, then you'll be important. Or you think the only way you can gain respect and value is if you have more money, a bigger house, nicer car, or brand name clothes. Or maybe you don't get the attention you feel like you deserve from your spouse so you 'harmlessly' flirt, constantly seeking after love, acceptance, and value from others. Or maybe you just don't feel significant. You've never had someone tell you they love you, or your constant searching for affirmation has left you exhausted and worn out. All of these emotions and insecurities are a result of fatherlessness ... because we don't know who our Daddy is.

We compare ourselves constantly because as long as we are doing 'better' than whomever, we feel alright. We care what other people think even if we don't really like those people. We humans are funny creatures. I mean, we don't even use plug-ins in our homes until we have company coming over so they think 'our' smell is better than it really is. As if our crap don't stink! I often times wondered why I had to clean my room when people were coming over. It's not like we were having dinner on my bedroom floor. But then again, these people don't know us too well. They can't find out about our junk until we know about theirs!

We laugh because it's true. We even do this in the church! We fight with our spouse on the way to church, and dad has his fly swatter on the dash just in case the siblings start fighting in the back. Bickering and complaints come flying from the back seat as dad throws out the empty threat, 'Don't make me pull over!' Then we file out of the van and act like everything is great even though the marriage is falling apart, we're two months behind on the mortgage, and we haven't told our wife about the promotion we didn't get. We put on our Sunday best and play the part of the perfect family, acting all proper as if the problems don't exist.

Hollywood doesn't need to have auditions for acting roles in movies, all they need to do is pick from the actors and actresses that show up in our churches each week. Isn't it funny how we call the church a hospital for the 'sick' yet once the 'sick' show up, they feel pressured to act a certain way as if they don't have issues. Only in church do we say we welcome everyone regardless of their wounds and then judge those wounds when they aren't stitched up as quickly as we think they should be. As if we have the authority to determine how grace is given and how much time it takes for Jesus to move in their lives.

Did you know the main reason for why many people didn't go to church this week is because they feel like they need to get right first? Get right; what? When did salvation ever become about getting right? When did being a follower of Jesus ever become about being a better person? As if we could earn the gift of salvation. Salvation wouldn't be called a gift from God if we could earn it! You can't earn a gift. This is why birthday presents don't make sense to me. Why in the world do I get a gift when it was my mother who pushed me out? I didn't do anything to be born, yet I'm the one receiving gifts every year on my birthday.

What is really under the surface that keeps us from being real? If God is omniscient (all-knowing) like we say He is, then He already knows your life is a disaster. He knows you're a mess! We know that God knows about our junk but we act like He doesn't. We rarely remember or dwell on what our Daddy calls us or how He views us. We refuse to believe God is excited to call us His sons and daughters. You may believe God is good, but when was the last time you believed God was good to you?

One of my favorite stories in the Bible is found in John

8. It's the story of a woman who is caught in adultery. The story begins with a group of people gathered around Jesus in the temple courts listening to Him teach. Then it gets interesting...

> At dawn He appeared again in the temple courts, where all the people gathered around Him, and He sat down to teach them. The teachers of the law and the Pharisees brought in a woman caught in adultery. They made her stand before the group and said to Jesus, 'Teacher, this woman was caught in the act of adultery. In the Law Moses commanded us to stone such women. Now what do you say?' They were using this question as a trap, in order to have a basis for accusing him. But Jesus bent down and started to write on the ground with his finger. When they kept on questioning him, he straightened up and said to them, 'Let any one of you who is without sin be the first to throw a stone at her." Again he stooped down and wrote on the ground. At this, those who heard began to go away one at a time, the older ones first, until only Jesus was left, with the woman still standing there. Jesus straightened up and asked her, 'woman, where are they? Has no one condemned you?' 'No one, sir,' she said. 'Then neither do I condemn you,' Jesus declared. 'Go now and leave your life of sin."

Now picture this for a minute. Before we talk about the woman, the Pharisees interrupt Jesus in the middle of His sermon! Jesus is teaching in the temple, also known as the church, and they bring Him a woman who was caught in the act of committing adultery. Can you imagine someone interrupting your pastor by bringing in a woman caught in the act of adultery? (And how often have you heard this story yet no one points out there was a guy involved, since adultery is not something you can commit alone. Plus, these Pharisees were either setting this woman up, or they knew this was going to happen because one of them was sleeping with her). Not only is that crazy to think about but this must have been completely embarrassing for this woman! I mean, not only is she caught in the act, she's then dragged in front of a bunch of people and judged, most likely still naked. Isn't it fascinating how our private issues never seem bad until they go public? I often find myself pointing out the junk in other people but I wouldn't want a video crew following me around 24/7 watching my every move.

In this Jewish culture, according to the law, this offense drew the death penalty. If one was caught committing adultery, a public stoning (and not a circle of people saying, 'puff puff pass') was the price to be paid. I picture the crowd growing with curiosity as people are sizing up the rocks they want to stone this woman with. The religious leaders speak up and they ask Jesus a trick question to try and trap Him in hypocrisy. See, if Jesus offers this woman grace, the religious leaders can accuse Him of breaking the Law of Moses but if Jesus sentences this woman to her death, they can accuse Him of breaking His own message of grace and love. It was the first ever catch 22 but Jesus knew what was going on. Instead of answering their question right away, He bends down and starts drawing in the sand. Now Scripture does not tell us what He wrote. We don't know if He wrote a phrase or if He was drawing pictures but if we focus our energy on what Jesus wrote we will miss the picture of the Gospel right here in this story. The Bible tells us that Jesus bent down to the dirt and then rose back up to respond to the religious leaders. Right here, we see the posture of Jesus and what He did on the cross. When we were caught in our unfaithfulness, Jesus came to Earth, died a sinners death, and then rose back up to bring His deliverance; and that is exactly what He is about to do for this woman. He stands up and instead of addressing their question, He asks them a question of His own: a question that causes people to reflect on their own hypocrisy. (As I said in the first chapter, have you ever noticed how Jesus almost always answers a question with a question? Yet so many Christians feel the need to win arguments or prove points when Jesus came to love people). Jesus says to everyone standing around Him with their stones in hand, *'Alright, who's up? If anyone here has never sinned, they can go first! Where is the perfect person?'*

I find it humorous as Scripture then tells us it's the older ones who start leaving first. As I grow older, I realize how much I don't know. I also am more conscious of how much I screw up. The longer you live, the more you sin. The older ones in the group are like, 'crap, this sucks'! And they start walking away first as if to say, 'yeah, I'm a mess too'! After a moment, we are told it is only Jesus and this woman standing there. Jesus looks to the woman and asked her if anyone has condemned her. She replies, 'no one'… "Then neither do I condemn you," Jesus declared. "Go now and leave your life of sin." What an incredible picture of grace.

Have you ever noticed when sinners got around Jesus they never felt condemned? We often bring people to church and instead of showing them the grace of God, all we want to do is point out their sin and show them how wrong they are. We watch movies about love triangles and people having affairs and then we get so disappointed when celebrities actually act it out in real life. We shame people we've put on pedestals who don't live by the standards we believe they should live by and we are so quick to throw rocks instead of offer grace. Yet the whole time, Jesus is trying to get us to understand that He loves us in spite of our sins. He forgives and restores. He removes all of our shame and He calls us His beloved!

There is also something extremely interesting in this story; something so clear about our identity as children of God. Did you notice throughout this whole story in John 8 that Jesus did not call this woman an adulterer? He never mentioned her specific sin. He accepted and loved her first before He instructed and challenged her. In fact, as I've studied the Bible, I've noticed that when Jesus does most of His miracles we are rarely given people's names. For example, the lame beggar who gets lowered by his four friends through the roof, the blind man who receives sight, the man with the withered hand, the woman with the blood issue for 12 years, the man with leprosy, the demon-possessed boy, or Peter's sick mother-in-law, etc. (Side note: most scholars believe the reason Peter denied Jesus three times is because Jesus healed his mother-in-law. Just kidding). All throughout the miracles of Jesus, we are only given people's gender and condition. We love to talk about people and their circumstances, sicknesses, or limitations. It is a part of our human nature to identify people by their issues, so much so that we actually turn our issues into our identity. We become known for our struggles instead of known as children of God. We label people by their mistakes or sins. We say things like that guy struggles with lust or he's a porn addict. That girl abuses drugs or alcohol. She's a gossip. He's divorced. She had an abortion, etc. We can't stop talking about our shortcomings! We focus so much on our sins we can't focus on our Savior anymore. We even do this from the pulpit. We talk so much on sins and spiritual disciplines that we forget to simply focus on the God who loves us in spite of ourselves. Do we realize the only way to grow in our relationship with God is to realize how much He really loves us? Do we realize the more we focus on Jesus, the less we will sin? One of my best friends and worship pastor at Cornerstone Church is Reggi Beasley, and he always says this quote when someone asks about the severity of sin. He says, "I'm not trying to be sin conscious, I'm trying to be Savior conscious." So many times I find myself saying I have to do this or that better; I have to stop doing this sin or that sin and the whole time my focus is still on my sin. Jesus is bigger than our sin. We'll be surprised how often we find ourselves sinning less when our focus is simply on Jesus and how much He loves us.

Truth is, we must quit focusing on our weaknesses. It is hard to love Jesus when we are so consumed with our struggles. In fact, most believers can't stop talking about sin because it's all we focus on. We talk more about our past instead of talking about the God who already dealt with it. Recently, I was checking out a local college ministry when I got into a conversation with one of the interns. He talked about his life and love of God but over the course of about five minutes, his main focus was one thing that he struggled with which caused frustration in the way he did ministry. He talked about how easily he gets discouraged and how it affects him. He probably said the word 'discouraged' seven times, and I didn't really pay attention until later when one of our team members said, 'Did you notice how many times that guy talked about being discouraged?' Well of course he struggles with discouragement, he kept focusing on it and speaking it over his life. I remember driving home that evening and thinking about this whole discouragement thing because truth be told, it was something I struggled with. I thought: If God is the encourager, comforter, and provider, why do I allow the devil to discourage me? Light bulb! Why in the world was my focus on my struggle? Why was I speaking death over my life without even realizing it? So many times in my life I do this to myself. Maybe for you it's an addiction, a sin, or a way of thinking. Your focus soon becomes more about your sin than your Savior. God is a greater Savior than you are a sinner. Quit focusing on your struggles because the more you focus on Jesus, the less you will sin. The Christian life is supposed to be a constant celebration. The beauty of Christ is incredible, and we are invited to be obsessed with Jesus, not our sin. Obsessed with the joy only Christ can give. Obsessed with the fact that our sin has already been paid for, in full.

God motivates us through His acceptance, grace, and love. He never uses anger, shame, guilt, or condemnation to motivate us to follow Him. I've heard pastors try to explain how guilt is a good thing. They say things along the lines of, 'It lets you know there is a problem that needs to be fixed'. I've even heard a guy relate guilt to a broken bone, saying the pain is letting you know you need to get something fixed. However, guilt is something God never uses. Guilt is a tool used by the devil to shame people into trying harder and doing better. John 3:18 and Romans 8:1 both say that in Christ there is no more shame or condemnation. So why do many Christian circles use it to motivate people into a relationship with Jesus?

Do we realize that as children of God we live in a constant state of forgiveness? Let's picture the Stauros again for a minute. If you didn't physically exist when Jesus died on the cross, yet God forgave the sins of the entire world in that moment, how many of your sins were forgiven? The answer is ALL! So if all of my sins were forgiven when Christ died on my behalf, that means my past, present, and future sins are completely forgiven. Even the sins I forgot about are forgiven. In Christ, you don't have to be identified by your mistakes, issues, or sins anymore! Jesus didn't know the woman in John 8 as an adulterer nor did He even call her one. He wasn't interested in condemning her past; He wanted to rescue her future! He loved her. He approved of her. He had already forgiven her. Jesus doesn't even know us by our sins. He knows us as His sons or daughters and He wants to rescue us from shame and condemnation and show us our true identity in Him. He wants to prove how loving He is and He does that by motivating us through pure, unadulterated acceptance and grace, regardless of our circumstances and choices. My love for God is a response to His great love for me.

I never really understood Matthew 3 until I began soaking in this message of sonship. Jesus comes to be baptized by John the Baptist. As Jesus comes up out of the water, the Scripture reads, "A voice from heaven said, 'This is my Son, whom I love; with Him I am well pleased.'" At this point in Scripture, Jesus has yet to do any miracle. He hasn't healed anyone, raised anyone from the dead, or met the needs of one person! Before Jesus did anything great, God said He was well pleased with Him. What an incredible picture of the reality of God's love. Jesus didn't have to do anything and God the Father was still proud of Him. The same is true for us. When was the last time you heard someone tell you God is proud of you? It doesn't matter what you've done or what you will do, God is well pleased with you! In my Bible, I have actually substituted Jesus' name with my name so that it reads, "This is my son Cory, whom I love, with him I am well pleased." This is an encouraging reality of how much God really loves every one of us!

We can smile at the understanding of God's incredible love and grace towards us. However, I brought up the end of Matthew 3 so that we can talk about what happens immediately following in Matthew 4. Right after Jesus is baptized and we hear what the Father says about Him, Jesus goes into the wilderness to fast for 40 days and 40 nights. Now notice Satan doesn't tempt Jesus until the last day of His fast. Often times, the devil comes to tempt us right before some of our biggest breakthroughs; if only we knew our true identity as sons and daughters even in the midst of temptations. Three times Satan tempts Jesus and all three times he starts off with the same phrase, "If you are the Son of God..." Satan is attacking the very identity that God the Father had spoken over His Son just a couple verses before. Satan tries to get Jesus to take His eyes off of His identity, the identity of God's 100% approval of Him. Satan tries to get Jesus to seek validation in other ways as if He needs the validation of anyone besides His Dad's! And Satan tries to do the same thing with us today. He tries to get us to find validation in materialistic things, people, and ourselves. He throws shame, guilt, and condemnation at us in an attempt to make us feel worthless, useless, and unloved. He doesn't want us to realize that as sons and daughters, God already approves of us. That God loves us, desires us, calls us worthy and righteous because of our belief in His Son, and empowers us to make His name famous. Satan will do whatever he can to make you doubt the reality of God's love and it starts with attacking our identity as sons and daughters.

What would happen if Christians really understood the power we have in the name of Jesus? What would happen if we understood our identity as God's children? Our staff talks about this a lot, the fact that Satan has no original thought. He's manipulative and his only way to attack us is by twisting God's truth. I remember the first time I heard Reggi preach this phrase, "Satan can only speak against what God has spoken for us." Understanding that sentence will give you great confidence in the real power of God. Think about this. God approves of His Son before He does anything great and the first thing Satan tries to do is take Jesus' eyes off this identity. Satan tries to get Jesus to find approval by doing something to prove His worth instead of resting in His Father's approval. The enemy does this with us all day long. He tries to get us to do religious deeds in order to earn love when we already have the love of God. He tries to get us to earn salvation when all you have to do is believe. He tries to remind us of our past when all you have to do is remind the devil of his future.

Satan may bring back our past to get us off track but that is not who we are anymore! He may know our history but he doesn't know our destiny because Christ is greater (1 John 4:4) and Christ lives in us! When we understand that there is nothing we can do to earn God's love - when we realize He is proud of us - when we realize we're a child by birth not by worth, it changes the course of our lives forever. Our sins don't define us. What we've gone through doesn't define us. The only thing defining us is what Jesus did on the Stauros for us! Now He resides in us, and everything that God the Father calls Jesus, He now calls us. God calls us worthy, righteous, and complete in Him! This is our identity.

Just like the religious leaders in John 8, you have two options as a believer: You can either offer grace like you have been given or you can throw rocks like a Pharisee. Identity in Christ is grasped when you understand that you cannot love better until you realize how loved you are! If God's grace wasn't sufficient, Paul wouldn't have said so in 2 Corinthians 12:9. This grace is amazing! This grace is what actually causes spiritual growth. If you want other areas in your life to line up with Scripture, you must focus on the grace of God. It's not about keeping records or statistics; it's about falling in love with a God who is unconditionally in love with you!

Romans 12:2 is another one of those verses that came to life when I began to understand grace and sonship. When God says to be transformed by the renewing of your mind, what He means is to remind ourselves of our identity in Christ. It's not about focusing on sins, struggles, or our past. It's all about reminding ourselves that He loves us in spite of us. It's reminding ourselves that God makes us worthy, righteous, and complete in Him. It's reminding ourselves that God calls us a saint, not a sinner. It's reminding ourselves that we are sons and daughters of the living God!

Brennan Manning, an incredible man who preached the grace of God until he passed away a couple of years ago believes the Lord Jesus is going to ask us one question and only one question when we see our Maker face to face. He believes God will look at us and ask, "Did you really believe that I loved you? That I desired you? That I waited for you day after day? That I longed to hear the sound of your voice?" He goes on to preach that many of us who are so faithful in ministry and church attendance, will reply to the question with a heartbreaking 'no'. They'll say they heard incredible sermons and teachings and even believed it occasionally through life but they really just thought it was the Christian way of patting people on the back and cheering them on. And that is the difference between real believers and the many people who say they follow Jesus in our churches today.[3]

This is important for us to grasp because we are only going to be as big as our own concept of God. If we don't believe God can move mountains in our life, mountains are not going to move. Famous French philosopher Blaise Pascal said, "God made man in His own image, and man returned the compliment." We refuse to believe that God is really as loving as He says He is so we create a God in our own image. We have made God too small. Manning is quoted as saying, "No one can measure like a believer the depth and intensity of God's love but at the same time, no one can measure like a believer the effectiveness of our gloom, pessimism, low self-esteem, self-hatred, and despair that block God's way to us…We want God to be fussy, rude, legalistic, narrow-minded, judgmental, unloving, and unforgiving like we are." We as humans start to base our identity on how well we are doing spiritually rather than on what God has declared over us in Christ. We must relate to God in light of who He really is, not just who we think or hope Him to be. The more you dwell on the reality of God's love for you, the more passionate you'll become and sin won't be as attractive to you as it once was. My challenge to you comes in the form of how Brennan Manning closed one of his sermons when he said, "God dares you to trust that He loves you just as you are and not as you should be because you are never going to be as you should be!"[4]

As a youth pastor, it's heartbreaking to watch some students chase after things that don't really matter. They get wrapped up in their looks, grades, sports, who they date, where they work, and who they hang with. As they get older, they continue to find their worth in what they do rather than who God says they are. As I talk with Christians and listen to the words they use to describe themselves, I wonder how many actually believe they are children of God.

In Christ, I'm no orphan anymore, I'm a child whom He loves! My identity in Jesus means I am beloved (Jeremiah 31:3), a child of God (1 John 3:1), delighted in (Zephaniah 3:17), forgiven (1 Peter 2:24), washed clean (Isaiah 1:18), free (Galatians 5:1), a temple of the Holy Spirit (1 Corinthians 6:19), adopted into God's family (Romans 8:15), co-heir with Christ (Romans 8:17), righteous (2 Corinthians 5:21), new (2 Corinthians 5:17), a saint (1 Corinthians 6:11), set apart (1 Peter 2:9), an ambassador of Christ (2 Corinthians 5:20), a co-laborer (1 Corinthians 3:9), a sweet aroma (2 Corinthians 2:15), never alone (Deuteronomy 31:8), a masterpiece (Ephesians 2:10), wonderfully made (Psalm 139:14), bold (2 Corinthians 3:12), having guaranteed victory (Psalm 18:35), holding a secured future (Jeremiah 29:11), whole in Christ (Colossians 2:10). My identity isn't what people call me. It's what my Daddy calls me and He calls me son!

CHAPTER 4

LET'S GET NAKED

What comes to mind when I say chains? My first thought comes from a song by Ludacris. *Whips and chains, handcuffs, smack a little*...okay, I'm done. Then, I think of scenes from movies such as *300* when those massive beasts rip through the chains they are shackled with to fight against the Spartans. Or I think of my favorite actor, Jamie Foxx, in the role he played in *Django*. I also think about the Biblical stories of Paul and Silas when they are thrown into prison in Acts 16 and it wasn't until they started worshiping that their chains came loose. Whatever it is you think of, chains represent bondage, slavery, and all kinds of other negative connotations having to do with being held hostage.

I say it a lot throughout this book that God calls us sons and daughters. He does not call us slaves. He doesn't even call us servants. Before you start to throw Scripture out of context at me or argue against the example that Jesus set, let me explain how important this is for us to understand. Yes, Jesus set the example of serving others. In fact, He calls us to serve others in love constantly throughout Scripture; but He never specifically calls us 'servants'. He does use examples of apostles being known as servants to spreading the Gospel but never is this anyone's identity. When we believe our identity in Christ is that of a servant, we miss the revelation of what God truly calls us.

Bishop Jamie Englehart says it this way, "The Kingdom of God is not a Kingdom of servants. The Kingdom of God is a Kingdom of sons and daughters who choose to serve." God calls us TO serve, but He specifically calls us His children! Servanthood is not our identity, sonship is. There are far too many people who don't understand that God calls us His sons and daughters. When people start to serve without knowing their true identity, serving becomes something they feel like they have to do instead of realizing it is something they get to do. They get to be a part of something bigger than themselves. Serving then becomes about being recognized and when recognition doesn't come, the feeling of worthlessness starts to creep in. The joy of serving starts to fade and the calendar is now full of chores instead of opportunities. They begin to feel like they are being taken advantage of, and serving now becomes defined as something negative. All because they believed God calls them servants instead of knowing their identity as sons and daughters. When we start to base our identity on how well we are doing, it causes us to forget the truths on what God has declared over us in Jesus.

When we know we are called His children, serving becomes something we choose to do regardless of the recognition. We serve because we know we already please the

Father. We serve because we understand the ministry we are a part of is so much bigger than the part we play. We serve not to receive a reward, but because we already possess the reward. The reward is Jesus! Do we realize the reward we receive in heaven we already possess in Jesus right now? This is freeing! This will allow us to be saturated in the reality of God's amazing love, because we don't earn it. His love is freely given.

Jesus understood this principle. He isn't a servant; He's a son who chooses to serve. Understanding Jewish culture will bring the passage in John 13 to life. This is when Jesus washed His disciples feet. Jesus knew His identity as a son. He knew the power that He possessed. He recognized the authority that He had. So what does he do? He serves, not because He felt like he needed to but because He wanted to. In fact, Scripture records in verse 4 that Jesus took off his outer clothing. Those who were Jewish in this culture would have understood exactly what that meant. The one in charge in any given room would wear this outer clothing. It was a custom of authority. It not only symbolized authority but it showed power and demanded respect. Here, Jesus has the authority in the room and what does He choose to do? He humbles Himself as the leader and serves by washing their feet. Jesus left us an incredible example of what serving truly represents. We don't serve to gain power; we serve to show the power we possess in Jesus. We choose to serve simply because we love Jesus. We choose to serve because we know our identity regardless of what recognition comes from it. I've heard it said that the reason General George Washington was given so much power and authority was because he was so willing and ready to give it up. Do we serve to get or do we serve to give? Do we serve because it makes us feel good or do we serve because it is good? Do we serve because we feel like we have to or do we serve because we already know we are a part of the family? We are not servants! We are sons and daughters who choose to serve because our Father served us!

Let's talk about the phrase 'slaves for Christ'. Respected author and speaker John MacArthur has written books and sermons about Christians being called 'slaves for Christ'. I get it, it's in Scripture. In fact, the word slave is used over 130 times in the original Greek New Testament, and often translators have replaced the word 'slave' with 'servant'. Many people say they believe they're a slave to Christ, and multiple authors in Scripture even say they are bondservants (which means slaves) of Christ. Again, knowing and understanding context in Scripture will challenge a lot of what you hear from the Bible today.

Anything in Scripture must be read in its right context. It's important to know who the author is and who he was talking to. For example, Paul writes about being a slave to Christ to start off several of his letters but what you may not know is the context of why that was written. He was talking to a culture that understood slavery because most of the people and churches he met with either had slaves or had a slave mentality. They were slaves to sin. 2 Peter 2:19 says, "…people are slaves to whatever has mastered them." This is why Paul used the word slave or bondservant to show the authority that God has in the life of a believer. But Romans 6 is pretty clear as to why Paul keeps using this phrase 'slaves to Christ'. After stating that they are no longer slaves to sin but slaves to righteousness, he says in verse 19, "I am using an example from everyday life because of your human limitations. Just as you used to offer yourselves as slaves to impurity and to ever-increasing wickedness, so now offer yourselves as slaves to righteousness leading to holiness." His audience would have understood exactly what that meant because of their slave mentality. They understood the role of a master in the life of a slave or servant. With this being said, it is important to understand that God is Master and Creator, but how He relates to us now is very different than that of a slave. In fact, God doesn't call us slaves anymore. Galatians 4:7 says, "You are no longer a slave, but God's child." Galatians 5:1 says that because Christ has set us free, we are to stand firm and not allow ourselves to be burdened again by the yoke of slavery! This is sonship, not servanthood or slavery. Jesus didn't die so we could transfer jail cells. He died to set us free! The thought process of understanding sonship is very essential to Christian living because God doesn't want to be known as Master, He wants to be known as our Father. He invites us to call Him 'Daddy'!

Let's break down the difference between a slave mentality and a sonship mentality…

- Slaves have a Master and are driven by duties. Sons and daughters however, have a Father and are driven by devotion. They love because the Father first loves them.

- Slaves are poor for they do not own anything, and they have the attitude of doing things because they 'have to' or are forced to. Sons and daughters are rich because everything that Jesus has, is now credited to those who believe. Jesus in fact dwells INside of us. Everything the Father calls Jesus; He now calls us those same things.

- Slaves are only trying to please the Master to escape

punishment and they live in a constant state of fear. Sons and daughters understand they already please the Father and they have the approach of doing things because they 'get to'. They do good deeds not to earn anything but simply because they identify with the reality that God loves them regardless.

- Slaves are insecure, strive for praise, approval, and acceptance from people, and have no genuine motivation to serve. Sons and daughters are secure and rest in knowing they are totally accepted by God and justified by His grace. They serve because they are motivated by a sense of gratitude for being unconditionally loved by God.

- Slaves fight for recognition. Sons and daughters share the journey with each other while giving God the glory.

- Slaves feel like they must be 'holy' to earn the favor of God, which only produces shame and condemnation. Sons and daughters want to be 'holy' because they love the intimacy they have with a God who loves them even if they aren't.

- Slaves end up driving themselves with guilt as they constantly compare themselves to others. They seek comfort from counterfeit affections such as addictions, busyness, and activities based off a religious action or check-list mentality. Sons and daughters understand their value, importance, and worth in Christ and find their comfort in knowing they are always in the presence and love of God. My personal prayers lately have changed from, 'God, fill this place with your presence' to 'God, help me become more aware that I am always in your presence!'

- Slaves are always in competition with one another and get filled with jealousy at the success of their peers. Sons and daughters live with humility and are unified in spirit as they rejoice in the success of their peers.

- Slaves only look out for themselves and try to expose others in an attempt to make themselves look better by making others look worse. Sons and daughters seek to restore relationships in gentleness and are respectful, honoring, and gracious to all people regardless of their social standing.

- Slaves proceed with caution as performance determines the condition of their love. Sons and daughters proceed with grace and patience as the unconditional love of the Father determines the unconditional love given to others.

- Slaves live in bondage and fight for what they can get. Sons and daughters live in freedom and fight for what they can give knowing their inheritance as children of God.

- Slaves have a desire to be seen and heard as spiritually mature much like the Pharisees of Jesus' day. Sons and daughters have a desire to experience the Father's love on a daily basis and they passionately want to be a representative of that love to everyone they meet. As Jack Frost says, "Moving from slavery to sonship or daughterhood is a matter of reaching the place where you get up in the morning feeling so loved and accepted in your Father's heart that your whole purpose for existence becomes looking for ways to give that love away to the next person you meet."[1]

Getting rid of the slave mentality is a tough but important process. You don't have to look far into the life of the Israelites to see how their slave mentality killed them from enjoying the Promised Land. They were delivered but not free because of the way they thought. We find out in Deuteronomy 1:2 that it was only supposed to take the Israelites 11 days to get to the Promised Land. Yet, it took them 40 years because of their disobedience! Yes, they were free from slavery but they were not free of a religious mentality. When Moses led them out of slavery from Egypt, it didn't take long for the Israelites to complain. They even said in Exodus 14:12, "Didn't we say to you in Egypt, 'Leave us alone; let us serve the Egyptians'? It would have been better for us to serve the Egyptians than to die in the desert!" Then moments later, God does an incredible miracle and parts the Red Sea as they walk across on dry ground. In one day, the Israelites go from slavery to freedom after being enslaved for 400+ years. They were out of Egypt but they could not shake the slave mentality they carried.

In Numbers 11, the Israelites start to complain about the food. Again, complaining about the reality that God was providing manna miraculously each and every day, they start to desire the fish they ate in Egypt. It goes on to talk about their cravings for cucumbers, melons, leeks, onions, and garlic. Then two chapters later, they refuse to take the land God had promised them because of fear. So, they begin to rebel and desire to be back in the hands of the Egyptians again. The cycle is incredible, and many times I do this in my own thinking. We are free in Christ yet we go back to rules and laws. We think our behavior is what makes us righteous, yet our righteousness comes from our belief in Jesus! Dr.

Lynn Hiles says, "The Son of God became the Son of Man so the sons of men could become the sons of God."[2] By our beliefs we are made children of God. Satan wants us to doubt our sonship and daughterhood! We must renew our minds in how God actually views us. We might still be in the process but God is not done with us yet. *He is the author and finisher of our faith.* Do not go back to what is comfortable just because trusting God is tough and not always clear! Press on, for God loves His children!

In the garden when Jesus prayed, "Abba", something incredibly awkward must have taken place among the disciples. In English, we translate Abba to Father, but in the Jewish culture it was the term used by children. Children who are just beginning to speak rarely ever use the term "father", but almost always use the term "Dada" or "Daddy". When Jesus prayed to His Father, He called Him Daddy! The disciples must have been shocked by this term because they were under the Mosaic covenant; meaning they did not have direct access to God. They could only go to God once a year through the high priest. Jesus not only spoke directly to God, but He also called Him Daddy – the term used by children. Jesus understood His relationship with His Dad! He was showing the disciples that this was the relationship Father God had wanted with His sons and daughters all along. The finished work of the cross was the start of a new covenant: a covenant that allows us direct access to God and a covenant that now makes Father God our Daddy! It might sound awkward at first to call out to God using the term Dad or Daddy but try it. Daddy is longing to hear the voice of His kids! He's longing to embrace us with a hug, put us in His lap, and speak words of affirmation over our lives. Call on your Dad; He's waiting with love!

Beginning to understand our sonship or daughterhood will cause a shift in our lives because we will start to realize how amazing God's grace really is. It is pretty amazing that because we are considered sons of God, He has now also made us an heir. In fact, Romans 8:14-16 is clear about our sonship when it says, "For those who are led by the Spirit of God are the children of God. The Spirit you receive does not make you slaves, so that you live in fear again; rather, the Spirit you received brought about your adoption to sonship. And by him we cry, 'Abba, Father'. The Spirit himself testifies with our spirit that we are God's children."

Dr. Lynn Hiles is a pastor who has made an impact in the lives of several of the men and women who influence me. In his book *Unforced Rhythms of Grace*, he explains the reality that we are no longer called servants or slaves, but sons. He writes,

> "We have not received the spirit of bondage that operates through fear. We are not under the slave masters of Egypt. We have been delivered by the blood of the spotless Lamb! We are not simply serving God. We are now heirs of God. We have his DNA, his Divine Nature Attributes. We now have a life and not a law. Jesus arrived on the scene to set us free from the tyranny of having to serve because of fear of retribution. This time He was delivering them not from a physical bondage, but from a spiritual bondage called religion and its taskmaster of fear. The Sabbath was meant to remember how He brought us out. How did He bring us out? He brought us out by the blood of the spotless Lamb. The work is truly finished. We have come to a

perpetual rest because we dwell in Him who completely finished the work. My Sabbath day is more than a day of the week. It is a person! His name is Jesus…Love is much more powerful than law. Faith is much more motivating than fear. Relationship works far greater than rules. It is out of our relationship and learning from Him that He teaches us the unforced rhythms of grace."[3]

In the story of the prodigal son in Luke 15, we actually read a story of two prodigal sons, or even better – A loving Father! We will dive deeper into this passage later but what I want to focus on now is the second son; the son who never left in the first place and who faithfully served his father without ever turning his back. The first son runs off and squanders his wealth. Years later he comes back and his father throws him a massive party in his return. He puts on him a robe and a ring on his finger and they kill the fattened calf. They feast and celebrate well into the night. The second son, who is the oldest and wiser of the two, happens to walk by the party and asks a nearby servant what is going on. The servant informs him that his younger brother has returned and his father is throwing him the bash of a lifetime. In verse 28, it tells us that the oldest brother becomes angry and refuses to be a part of the party. So his father goes out to him and pleads with him. The son responds, "Look! All these years I've been slaving for you and never disobeyed your orders. Yet you never gave me even a young goat so I could celebrate with my friends. But when this son of yours who has squandered your property with prostitutes comes home, you kill the fattened calf for him!"

Wow, I've got to be honest. I have felt that way

sometimes too when I see other people having bigger and better stuff than me. I have allowed jealousy to change my attitude in a negative way before too. And to be honest, is the oldest son really out of line to have feelings like this? I mean come on, his younger brother was an idiot! But when we react like the oldest brother, we miss the message of grace and we miss the message of sonship.

So often we focus on the younger son, the son who leaves and lives in sin, but the oldest son plays a massive part in portraying how 'church people' today miss the grace of God. Many people do 'good deeds' so they can look at other people and say things along the lines of, 'I'm better than that person...'" We even compare ourselves to believers and say, "I'm a better Christian than them because they do that and I don't." Look at how the oldest son responds to his father; look at how he even views himself. He calls himself a slave and thought he could earn favor and earn material possessions. He himself had a slave mentality and only obeyed for personal gain. He didn't know his identity as a son and he allowed himself to sink into bitterness, hate, and despair.

Notice how the father responds in verse 31. He tells the oldest son that *everything he owns is already his*. Do we realize that everything our Father God owns is already ours? Do we realize that the grace God uses to bring us into His Kingdom is the same grace He offers us daily? Do we realize God still offers grace to those who think they are morally better than others? Do we realize God wants us to find our identity as sons and not as slaves or servants?

God is crazy about you. It is His kindness that leads us into a relationship with Him and it's His kindness that continues it. Let us never miss the reality of what our Daddy calls us. Let us never find ourselves in a slave mentality where we believe God should bless us because of our obedience. God blesses us simply because we are His children. He blesses us because of what Jesus has done. We must recognize that God doesn't need to do another thing for us than what He has already done through His Son Jesus on the cross. Everything else is a blessing straight from the very hands of God. You can't earn your righteousness; quit trying. Righteousness is credited to those who simply believe. Just rest in the peace of knowing that your Daddy loves you, He actually enjoys you, and He is excited to call you His own!

CHAPTER 5

SLAYING SANTA

My family has many traditions that we participate in. Traditions can be fun and bring us great joy. They also create fantastic memories. As I am writing this, Christmas is right around the corner and with Christmas comes many traditions within my family. We would all go out on the Friday after Thanksgiving to find the perfect, real Christmas tree (emphasis on real – who wants fake when you can get the real thing? I believe this applies to almost everything in life). Every year, I would watch my dad struggle to tie the Christmas tree to our vehicle. By the time we got home, I was exhausted from all his hard work. I would always find myself taking a nap the moment we got home, waking up hours later to find all the Christmas decorations up and ready to go. It's amazing how much work can get done while you're sleeping! I really don't understand why my family labels me as the lazy one; I like to think of myself as a genius.

Christmas Eve is one of my favorite days of the year simply because of our family tradition. I receive three gifts every year. The first one has to do with our gift exchange with my grandparents. I'm one of four boys who are all grown and equally immature. Our goal over the years has been to see who can get them the most inappropriate gift, simply to see their reaction as they open it. Watching my grandfather try to figure out how to properly use the shake weight will go down as one of my favorite memories of all time. The second gift is new pajama pants. My mom thinks I am too old for them, but every year I look forward to this gift. I love pajama pants and I love to wear them in public. I fit right in with everyone who shops at Wal-Mart. Don't judge me. The third gift is my favorite and something my family has been doing since I was born. Every year I receive a Christmas ornament, and it represents an event that impacted my life that year. When I relocated to the Louisville area, my parents got me a bourbon barrel ornament to represent my big move in 2012 (Kentucky is known for their bourbon). Now that I am living on my own, I have a shoebox of twenty-something ornaments representing milestones in my life.

Many traditions are good and I love the ones I celebrate in my life. But there are also bad traditions, and some that we no longer participate in because they ended up being disastrous. Have you ever had that 'thing' you and your family did and you claimed it was going to be a new family tradition yet everyone hated it? My dad used to put up a tent in our backyard on the last day of school for us to 'camp' in. It represented the start of summer and all the fun we were going to have. I don't know about you but I hate camping, especially camping in the back yard. I don't understand why people enjoy pretending to be homeless! This tradition quickly ended when I wet the tent and claimed it was just the morning dew. I'm only kidding, I think.

We all have traditions. Good traditions and bad traditions, but what I want you to grapple with now is the traditions you have in your faith - what it is you believe about God and the Bible and why. As a Christian, there are things I was taught growing up about the Bible that aren't necessarily true. For example, how many animals did Noah bring with him on the ark? We learn in Sunday School that Noah brought two animals of every kind onto the ark, yet when I actually read the story for myself in Genesis 7, I found something completely different. Genesis 7:2 actually tells us that God told Noah to take seven males and seven females of every kind of clean animal, etc. Yes, the animals enter the ark two-by-two according to Genesis 7:8-9, but there were actually 14 animals of every clean kind that entered the ark.

You might say that is a minor detail but the reality is, how many more 'truths' do you hear in sermons without checking for yourself? Just because someone is a Pastor or a Bible teacher, doesn't mean they always teach the Word of God accurately. Don't just take my word for it either, research for yourself. Just because I teach and write doesn't mean I'm always accurate. I try to be, but I'm human. Your Pastor is too, so give him or her the benefit of the doubt if they preach something out of context and offer them grace. However, don't just assume everything you hear is true.

Maybe you grew up with the tradition that Christianity is about religious duties or obeying specific laws. Unfortunately, it's a tradition that many Pastors preach when it comes to mandatory good deeds and other grace eroding sermons. In Matthew 15, we see the Pharisees questioning Jesus about breaking traditions in the Jewish culture. Jesus responds in verse 6 with a simple truth that deals with our traditional beliefs today. He said, "You nullify the word of God for the sake of your tradition." I really want us to think about the foundation or the roots of what it is we actually believe about God. What if some of the things we have been doing or believing isn't even what Jesus wants us to focus on?

Christianity is based on a worldview that many Christians do not hold. We see evil happening before our eyes and our first response is usually anger. We want revenge or justice yet the whole story about Jesus is one of love and grace. Yes, justice is good but justice isn't ours. Revenge isn't ours. That is up to God (Romans 12:19). Grace is so hard for us to understand because it goes against everything we are taught in our culture. In fact, we would never admit this, but many of us believers have moments where we believe in a doctrine taught in Buddhism and Hinduism. It's a doctrine of Karma – the belief that good things happen to good people and bad things happen to bad people. However, Karma is not how God operates.

When we are asking the wrong questions and thinking the wrong way, we end up believing Jesus came to make the rules harder. For example, the Sermon on the Mount recorded in Matthew 5-7, also known as the greatest sermon ever preached, is one of those stories that rarely gets preached accurately. Jesus is preaching to Jews under the Jewish law. He is preaching to a bunch of Pharisees who were justifying their actions through this checklist called the law (10 commandments plus 603 other laws they included to try to gain 'righteousness'). These Pharisees were looking at the law and claiming that because they didn't sleep with other dudes wives and/or murder people that they were doing pretty good. They were claiming a statement that many Christians claim today, a statement saying, "I'm a better Christian than you because you do that and I don't." Jesus wanted this audience to understand that if they wanted to live by the law, they couldn't pick and choose which laws to obey and justify themselves by. In the Pharisees own efforts to be good people, they redefined holiness so they could fulfill the law on their own, apart from a relationship with God. They justified themselves in their own eyes. This is why Jesus is quoted in this sermon as saying murder isn't just an action. He said, "If you hate someone you've just committed murder. If you've even lusted after a woman, you've just committed adultery." If you didn't understand context, you would believe Jesus just made the laws or rules harder. However, Jesus was proving that you can't justify yourself based on your own deeds. He wanted His audience to come to the end of themselves and discover grace through Him. He was explaining that obedience to the law does not save you, only trusting in Him does. He wants us to stop comparing ourselves and stop this checklist mentality. Jesus is saying we are all guilty of breaking this law, BUT I fulfilled this law on your behalf. Jesus set us free from the 'laws' to help us understand that it is only about Him; it is only about His grace. Jesus has set us free from trying to be good enough.

This checklist mentality is a tradition we must kill. But we also must kill some Christian clichés that so many people preach and so many people believe.

First, you can't get more of God. I can't tell you how often I hear it preached that all we need is more of God. The truth is, you either already have all of Him or you have none of Him. When you put your faith and trust in Christ, He gives you all of Him! He doesn't give you portions of Himself or wait for you to turn a certain age or gain a certain level of maturity before He gives you the rest of Him. It's all or nothing. I remember exactly where I was when the Lord first spoke this truth to me. It was my first full time gig as a youth pastor. I had been a part of ministries as an intern for 5 plus years but never had the authority or responsibility as the leader until the spring of 2012. I took about 25 students and leaders to a summer camp held at Liberty University and I was feeling the pressure of being 'in charge' for the first time. I was stressed, anxious, and just wanted to see God move among my students. I remember praying for each of my leaders and kids, praying over the seats, and praying for the camp as a whole. There were just over 2,000 people about to be rocked with the Gospel and I was stoked. I prayed these exact words, "God, I just want more of you. I want my students to want more of you. Reveal yourself to us this week." The auditorium soon became packed and the worship team came out and rocked the place with life-filled worship. Right in the middle of the first song the Lord impressed this on my heart, "You don't come to camp to get more of me, you come to camp and I get more of you." Hello! Do we realize how entertained we are in today's society? We have so much constant noise in our lives that it is so easy to tune out the voice of God. We start screaming at God to give us more of Him while He's been waiting for us to give Him all of ourselves. We already possess every aspect of God the Father. Could it be that God is waiting for us to recognize it? Colossians 2:9-10 says, "For in Christ all the fullness of the Deity lives in bodily form, and in Christ you have been brought to fullness. He is the head over every power and authority." That word fullness means we're not missing any part of the person of Christ. We only have to activate His fullness in our lives and wake up to the reality that we already possess everything we need right now to make an impact in our area of influence.

Second, Emmanuel doesn't just mean God with us. Emmanuel actually means God within us. We say this a lot at our church, "A quiet church is a dead church and we're not a dead church." We celebrate week in and week out because the victory is already ours in Christ. The living God actually lives INside of us. That is something to get hyped about because there is no evil power bigger than our God, who rules and reigns IN us! If Christ is IN you, you're spiritually united with Jesus (Romans 6:5) and seated on the lap of the Father (Ephesians 2:6, Revelation 3:21). We are actually one in Spirit with the Lord (1 Corinthians 6:17). As we realize this union with Christ, every motive we have will begin to change and we'll begin to see that living the Christian life is really just being ourselves! I heard a pastor once say, "Nothing that you have is something that God needs, but everything you have is something He can use!" Everything you need is already in you; you just have to believe it! 1 John 4:4 tells us that the One who is IN you is greater than the one who is in the world. Therefore, the search for more is over. No more hungering, no more thirsting, no more waiting for more of God. The spiritual life we carry within us is the Teacher Himself, the risen Christ who is seated on the throne with God. If you have Jesus, you truly lack nothing!

Third, righteousness is not given or taken from us based on our behavior. In Christ, righteousness is already ours based on belief not behavior. Righteousness means nothing for us today unless we own it. If God is righteous and He lives in me, I'm righteous in Christ. If God is complete and He lives in me, I'm complete in Christ. If God is perfect and

He lives in me, I'm perfect in Christ. Romans 4:3 tells us, "Abraham believed and it was credited to him as righteousness." So how do we become righteous? By believing God to be who He says He is. By believing God when He says He loves us in spite of our actions. By believing God when life falls apart and circumstances don't make sense. By believing God to provide when our finances don't line up. By believing God is enough! Because I am in Christ, God now sees me according to how Jesus has lived, not by how I act. Let this reality sink in. In Christ, God no longer sees me as a sinner saved by grace; He now sees me as a saint saved by grace. Regardless of my situation, He sees Jesus in me; He sees the righteousness of Christ. The life Christ lived on Earth has now been credited in full to those who believe.

Fourth, we don't live by the commandments under the old covenant. The commands of God are two-fold, not 10, not 613, just two. We read verses like John 14:15 which says, "If you love me, obey my commands." We think that God's commands refer to His 10 commandments, but understanding law vs. grace, old covenant vs. new covenant will help you better understand what God means when He says to obey His commands. The sole purpose of the 10 commandments in the life of a believer today is to point us to Jesus. This is why the 10 commandments are used in evangelism. They are to show us that we are all criminals and in need of a Savior. That is why it is so hard for people to receive Jesus, because He is the cure to a disease most people don't believe they have. If we don't understand that without Christ we are evil at the core, we will never grasp the reality that the Gospel is actually good news. Jesus fulfilled the law (10 commandments) when He died on the cross. Therefore, when we look at the 10 commandments, we should praise Jesus because He fulfilled those laws on our behalf. We don't live by the 10 commandments today. We live by two commands this side of the cross. These are the commands written on our hearts (Hebrews 10:16 and 1 John 3:23). The first is to believe God is who He says He is. The second is to love. Some claim the greatest command given in Matthew 22 is to love God with all your heart, mind, strength, and soul and the second is like it, to love your neighbor as yourself. But what they don't know is Jesus was actually quoting the law to the Jewish leaders. If you read the passage again, you will see Jesus is simply answering their question, not giving a command. The Jewish leaders were more focused on the traditions of their religious duties than resting in the peace and hope that God provides. They were promoting a moral code of conduct; Jesus is promoting love and life. In John 13:34, Jesus says, "A new command I give to you, to love as I have loved you." That command is very different from loving your neighbor as yourself. Now, God calls us to love as He loves us. And He loves us with unconditional grace and love. Someone living under the law would say something along the lines of, "So we can murder someone now since we don't live under the 10 commandments?" The answer is no, you missed it. When we live by these two commands: believing God in all circumstances and loving as God loves us, it's impossible to murder. Think about it. The commands of God are not as hard as most Christians make them seem. How different would our lives be if we just believed God is who He says He is? What would happen if we really believed God when He tells us He loves us and is proud of us? How many lives would be changed if we loved all people regardless of what they bring to the table? We can love God because He first loved us. We can love people because the good news of the Gospel is actually good news. As Gregory Boyd says, "Every truth, every deed, every teaching is reduced to nothing more than religious noise when it isn't placed under and clothed in the commandment to love."[1]

Fifth, the power of the Gospel is not activated when we pray, give, and behave like good people. Rather, it is released as we believe it. Genuine growth occurs as we absorb the truth about who we already are and what we already possess in Christ. We shouldn't sit around and wish for more cleansing, or more Holy Spirit, or more of whatever popular teaching says is lacking in us. We have everything we need right now for a godly life. We have an unshakable kingdom, an eternal covenant, and every spiritual blessing. We are complete in Christ and lack nothing. The only logical response is to spend our lives reminding each other of these extraordinary truths and give thanks to our Father daily! Pastor Andrew Farley says, "Merely going through the motions of imitating Christian activity pales in comparison to the experience of having Christ's life naturally flow from your personality!"[2] As we believe, and realize the power of God is actually INSIDE of us, we will start a movement for the Kingdom that will not be stopped. We will actually start to look more like Jesus and compassion will fill our lives and force us to reach out to people with love.

Finally, we already posses the prize we'll have in Heaven because the prize is Jesus! I hear all kinds of Christians joking around about how their actions gain or remove jewels from their crowns in Heaven, or that their good deeds earn some kind of Heavenly reward. We throw around words like treasure, prize, or reward as if our good works produce bigger mansions for us to live in when we get to Heaven. I don't know where we learned this teaching because it's not in the Bible. As I said in chapter 3, do we realize the reward we receive in Heaven is Jesus? And if Jesus lives IN us, then we already have our reward. In fact, you will never find the plural use of the word 'reward' anywhere in the New Testament. Paul spoke of a reward or prize in running the race and reaching the end, but what is this prize he is talking about? In Matthew, you read of Jesus saying to store up treasures in Heaven, but as I've studied, treasures aren't rewards. Actually, you don't earn treasures at all; you find them. And once you find them, you can either invest it or leave it as if you never found it. Farley says, "As humans, we always seem to be looking for a punishment or reward-based motivation to keep our behavior on track."[3] And as I've talked to believers, this seems to be a common factor. Farley goes on to say, "God doesn't want us to think and act in certain ways because we're seeking to accumulate heavenly merchandise. Just as Paul was willing to lose all things for the sake of knowing Christ, we too should make it our agenda to know Him! For more wealth in Heaven? No, we want to know Christ simply because it's the greatest thing going on planet Earth."[4] Wow. The real question for us today is, is Jesus enough? Frankly, the reward is Jesus. A life filled with unconditional love, sufficient grace, and a reality that in Christ we are perfect, worthy, righteous, and completely forgiven. A life with Christ means we are now saints...saints saved by grace. The reward is allowing Jesus to live through our lives in the here and now. Will we store up treasures, or should I say an attitude of love (actions) that endures forever, or will we pursue the unfulfilling success of 'dead works' that don't earn us 'jewels'? The choice is yours, the reward is now!

In 2 Corinthians 4:7-9, Paul writes "But we have this

treasure in jars of clay to show that this all-surpassing power is from God and not from us. We are hard pressed on every side, but not crushed; perplexed, but not in despair; persecuted, but not abandoned; struck down, but not destroyed." This treasure IN jars of clay. What does that mean? It's actually quite simple; Jesus is the treasure, we are the jars of clay. Jesus living IN average and ordinary people. Jesus is IN us and if Jesus is IN us, we are capable of extraordinary things. In fact, 'all-surpassing power' in the Greek means extremely extraordinary or surpassing excellence. So, Jesus lives IN average, ordinary people. But because Jesus lives IN us, we now become extremely extraordinary or surpassing in excellence because He is IN us. We now have power in the name of Christ. Therefore, we are able to conquer any trial, hardship, discouragement, shame, or any other struggle the devil throws our way. We may be struck down, but we are not destroyed! This is what I want people to understand because trusting in Jesus does not make life perfect. If we sell people on the idea that Jesus makes life perfect, when their life falls apart, so will their faith. Jesus gives us the ability to endure any circumstance because in His power we have strength. The reward is the life of no fear, living in peace and hope, knowing Christ has conquered all things! Jesus brings Heaven to Earth! Our reward is the best life now, His life living through us! A life of love and grace!

CHAPTER 6

LIKE AN ANGEL

What do you think of when you hear of the devil? Let's face it, our first thought when talking about Satan is usually something along the lines of evil, sin, temptation, death or hate. My whole life I was taught to believe Satan was one of the three archangels mentioned in Scripture, and before he was kicked out of Heaven, he was the angel in charge of worship. These views of the devil supposedly come from Ezekiel 28 and Isaiah 14, but recently I was challenged on these interpretations. I'm not going to spend this chapter dissecting these passages but it seems like we have wrongly read Satan into those chapters. Then, Revelation 12 tells us the story of the woman and the dragon (Satan); that a war in Heaven broke out between Michael and his angels vs. the dragon and his angels. This story is interesting because it tells us Satan and his angels *lost their place in heaven* and were *hurled to the Earth*. But to say Satan and his angels were first God's angels is what we call eisegesis (reading something into a text). So the question remains, how and why is Satan in Heaven? Great question. I have the same question when we find Satan before the Lord in Heaven in the book of Job. Regardless, you won't find any Scripture informing us that Satan was one of God's angels, let alone the angel in charge of worship.

In 2 Corinthians 11:14 it says, "Satan masquerades as an angel of light." Notice it doesn't say he is an angel but rather, he impersonates an angel. Satan actually has the power to disguise himself LIKE an angel. His lies won't always seem like lies because they sound good, tolerant, and politically correct but just because something sounds nice doesn't make it true. Hip-Hop artist Lecrae says it this way, "A wolf is no less a wolf because he's dressed in sheepskin and the devil is no less the devil because he's dressed as an angel."[1] There is no better tactic for Satan than to first tempt us into thinking sin isn't that bad; then to flood us with guilt, shame, and condemnation after we sin, masquerading as the Holy Spirit, condemning believers into thinking they aren't saved or worthy of being used for God's Kingdom. Understanding our sonship is extremely important here because guilt, shame, and condemnation are not from God.

Today, we know the devil is evil and wants nothing more than for people to live in pain with bitterness, unforgiveness, and hate. His schemes are wicked and he works through shame, discouragement, pride, and fear. He knows shame and condemnation will keep people from understanding and living in the grace God provides. He knows discouragement can derail us from doing what God has called us to do. He knows pride can destroy us from the inside out and keep us from seeking God daily. He knows fear can keep us captive and cause us to live with worry and anxiety without trusting in the Creator. However, these four specific tactics that Satan uses can be conquered! Shame is defeated with grace. Discouragement is defeated through praise. Pride is defeated through prayer. Fear is defeated by knowing and standing on the Word of God. In Scripture, we know the devil lies (John 8), tempts (Matthew 4), disguises (2 Corinthians 11), sifts – which means to break down so finely that it cannot be used anymore (Luke 22), snatches (Luke 8), blinds (2 Corinthians 4), enslaves (2 Timothy 2), and destroys (1 Peter 5). But what if our knowledge of Satan and our lack of knowledge of the Holy Spirit have driven us into a state of misunderstanding our power in Christ?

The same power that raised Jesus from the grave actually lives inside of us! Satan's goal is to obliterate us, and the last thing he wants us to understand is the power we have in the name of Jesus. When it comes to spiritual warfare, especially for teenagers, it's easy to put the devil into one of two categories. We either fear him and put an emphasis on his 'power', or we completely ignore the existence of his reality. Both are extremely dangerous! Ephesians 6 is one of my favorite passages of Scripture and it talks about putting on the full armor of God. What that really means is knowing our sonship or daughterhood and memorizing Scripture; but have you ever noticed the 'armor' described in this passage? Every part of this armor protects the 'soldier' from head to toe but it only covers the front. All of this armor actually leaves the 'soldiers' backside completely exposed. In times of war throughout the life of Saul and David, this kind of armor was used to discourage any warrior from fleeing the battle. If one fled, they most likely would be killed because nothing protected their back. These soldiers understood this! The armor they wore was designed to encourage these soldiers to face their opponent head on! The same is true in Christianity. God gives us the power of His Word and when we put it to heart, standing firm in the Lord, we can stand our ground and face the devil head on. The moment we turn and flee in fear is the moment Satan defeats us. Be encouraged, we have the ability to face our opponent head on as we put on the full armor of God! Understanding Scripture gives us the ability to see right through Satan and his evil schemes, knowing Jesus defeated him on the cross. We must become people who seek and memorize what the Bible actually says, instead of believing everything we hear because it sounds good. When we let the Word of God manifest in our hearts, it changes the way we view life. It changes the way we view people. It even changes the way we view Satan.

Do you ever wish Jesus was physically present with you at all times? I think it would totally help prevent us from sinning if Jesus in human form was walking with us everywhere we went! Yet, understanding the role of the Spirit in our daily lives, reminding ourselves of His presence withIN us is actually what will help prevent us from sinning. We have greater power living withIN us in the Spirit than we would if Jesus was physically standing with us.

Many believers think it's the job of the Holy Spirit to convict people. In John 16, we see Jesus telling His disciples He had to go so the Holy Spirit could come and dwell within us. According to John 16, the Holy Spirit is our counselor, helper, comforter, and advocate. He guides us into all truth (John 16:13). He prays on our behalf (Romans 8:26). He testifies to us concerning our identity as children of the living God (Romans 8:16). Yet, He does not convict us like many people think He does. Why would the Holy Spirit be convicting believers of sin if sin was taken care of on the cross? In fact, there is only one place in Scripture where the word convict is used in the same sentence as the Holy Spirit. In John 16:8, most translations use the word 'prove' or 'convict' to talk about the Holy Spirit's job, but the word used in the original Greek translates the word 'prove' to 'convince'! Using the word convince here is very important in understanding the job of the Holy Spirit in our lives because the Holy Spirit is not here to convict us of sin. The job of the Holy Spirit in the life of believers is to convince us of our righteousness in Christ. When we are tempted with sin, the Holy Spirit withIN us is there to convince us that we are better than sin because we have Jesus. We don't need moments of pleasure to satisfy us because we are satisfied in Christ. In the life of non-believers, the Holy Spirit is there to convince them they need Jesus. That life in Christ is better than any lie they believe. That Jesus is enough and will satisfy their souls. It's time to listen to the voice of the Spirit, for He is here to convince us of our identity as sons and daughters of the most high King.

Another sometimes confusing tactic Satan uses to cause all kinds of fear in the life of a believer is around the question of God's sovereign will. For me personally, the most common question I get from teenagers is how can they know God's will and stay in it. They sometimes overflow with so much worry and anxiety that they believe their decisions can remove the will of God from their lives. For the record, God's will is less about what you're doing or where you are and so much more about who you are. It is God's will for your life that you know your identity as a son or daughter. When you know you're a part of the royal family, you live like royalty. Johnnie Moore says, "God's will is more about you going until He stops you than waiting until He starts you."[2] According to Ecclesiastes 9:10, WHATEVER your hand finds to do, do it with all your might. Again in Colossians 3:17, WHATEVER you do, do it all in the name of Jesus. In essence, WHATEVER you choose to do, that is your mission field! Do everything with a desire to expand the Kingdom of God. I'll break it down in Scripture even further. This list was given to me by my youth pastor, Jack Janigian, and it helped me tremendously…

It is God's will that you are…
- Saved (1 Timothy 2:3-4)
- Spirit-controlled (Ephesians 5:17-20)
- Sanctified (1 Thessalonians 4:3-7)
- Submissive (1 Peter 2:13-15)
- Suffer for doing good (1 Peter 3:17-18)
- Supplication – to rejoice, pray, and give thanks (1 Thessalonians 5:16-18)

In other words, if you believe in Jesus, are led by the Spirit, living a life of purity (thank God for grace), submitting to authority (even that teacher you dislike), stand up for your faith, and rejoice always despite the season of life you're in; you will be doing the will of God. Therefore, whatever you choose to do in life, if Jesus is at the center, you are doing the will of God. Again, it's more about who you are than what you do because when you know you're a child of the King, you will live like it. Psalm 37:4 says, "Take delight in the Lord, and He will give you the desires of your heart." This verse doesn't mean that God will give you what you want. It means that when you're following and trusting God, He will give you His desires. Your desires will begin to shift and you will care more about growing the Kingdom of God than the selfish desires you may want.

After God's will, I usually receive a question around how to make a decision in life, such as where to go to school, what career to pick, who to date, which job should I take, should I move my family, etc. The best way to go about making a decision in my opinion is the three-step process I learned from my friend Reggi Beasley…

When making a decision…
1. Does it TESTIFY of God?
2. Does it fall in line with the TALENTS I've been blessed with?
3. Do I have the TIME to do it well, without neglecting a prior commitment?

After answering those questions, move forward if…
1. The timing is right
2. It makes sense and I have God's peace
3. It's in line with the Word of God

At the end of the day, you the reader need to know that the decisions you make in life aren't blessed…you are blessed! God's anointing never leaves you no matter where you go in life. Isaiah 30:21 tells us whether we go to the left or the right that God is with us each step of the way. So be encouraged, the King isn't waiting for us to get to a specific place. He's waiting for us to realize how important we are to Him and how much He cares about us. He's waiting for us to start knowing our identity in Him, our identity as sons and daughters. He is well pleased with us. He is proud of us and He wants us to know how much He loves us. When we start to look for love in the wrong places, we forget the reality of our identity as God's children. J.D. Greear says, "When Satan takes our eyes off of the declaration spoken over us in the Gospel, we lose the security and satisfaction we have in the loving approval of our heavenly Father...The gateway is then opened for all the other temptations."[3] This is why knowing who God says we are will prevent us from doing things we know we shouldn't.

This is one of the devil's greatest weapons against us: making us forget our identity in Christ. He does this by reminding us how we've messed up and condemns us by making us feel like we aren't approved by God. But Romans 8:1 and John 3:18 tells us that there is no condemnation in Christ. Satan tries to convict us of our sin and tell us the sacrifice Jesus made on the cross to remove all condemnation wasn't enough. We feel so much shame that we believe the only thing the Holy Spirit does is convict or remind us of sin when in fact it is our enemy doing that. I stated earlier in Chapter 3 that Satan has no original thought. Understanding this truth will set us free. Satan is not a creator but a perverter. He only has counterfeits. He is the king plagiarizer. He takes good thoughts and redirects them into his own purpose and can only speak against what God has spoken for us. But knowing the Spirit is here to convince us of our sonship or daughterhood in the Kingdom of God is what really causes an inward change. Truth is, no one measures up to the standards of God, and over time you may start to believe the lie that you aren't good enough to follow Jesus. But the Spirit is here to remind us of our Champion. He's here to remind us that Jesus wants us! And He's convincing us we don't need what the world has to offer anymore. As Jack Frost says, "It is impossible to be free as long as your thoughts and attitudes are in agreement with the father of lies."[4]

When we have the Spirit in us, we become ALIVE in Christ. Now I know nothing about hunting, but living in the Louisville area, I am surrounded by some die-hard hunters. Last time I checked, shooting something that is already dead isn't a big deal. Actually, most wouldn't brag about the 10-point rack hanging on the wall unless they were the one who shot it. This is what makes Satan a smart hunter. He's not trying to 'kill' people he sees as 'dead'. He's trying to condemn and kill those who are alive in Christ. Satan's best attempt at making us fall is to have us question the reality that God actually calls us His sons and daughters. This happened in Genesis 3 when Adam and Eve ate of the fruit they weren't supposed to eat. I've heard pastors describe this as Satan trying to get Eve to doubt God's word and he tries to do the same with us today. However, the language used in this passage is actually quite interesting. Yes, Satan does try to make us doubt God in His goodness, faithfulness, and love but understanding the Hebrew language will bring the truth of what Satan really did in this passage of Scripture. When Satan said in Genesis 3:1, "Did God really say…", it wasn't so much to make Eve doubt as it was Satan straight up mocking God altogether. Satan knows anything that is mocked will be mistrusted. This is why when something or someone is mocked in our culture, it's all we can think about. For example, the Baltimore Ravens won the Super Bowl a couple years back. The week leading up to the Super Bowl, SNL did a skit mocking Ray Lewis with Kenan Thompson as he dressed like him, acted like him, and talked like him. The skit was hilarious and spot on. But when the Ravens won the Super Bowl, they interviewed Ray Lewis as it was his last game before retirement. As Ray started speaking, wearing his Psalm 91 shirt and praising God all throughout his interview, I couldn't help but laugh. Even though I was agreeing with what he was saying and proud of his public confession of his love for God, I was laughing because I couldn't stop thinking about Kenan Thompson and his excellent impersonations of the hall of fame linebacker. I couldn't focus on what was really being said because earlier that week he had been mocked. This is exactly what Satan was doing in the Garden when he tempted Eve with that simple question, "Did God really say…"

Satan and Eve both knew exactly what God had said. Satan wasn't trying to confuse Eve by asking her whether or not God really said what He said. Satan was mocking God! Imagine this sentence said with a sarcastic tone and an arrogant laughing voice…Did God really say that?! HA! Satan knew if he could get Eve to think God's command was silly, she would feel like God was restricting her and give in. And this is the cycle of human life. Satan constantly attacks us to make us think that God's boundaries are limiting our freedom and fun. Yet, as I've grown older, it's easy to understand that boundaries protect us from things we don't fully understand or keep us from sins we will regret. To start, let's talk about sex. In our culture today, sex is abusive. We are told we need to sleep with as many people as possible and figure out who we are sexually compatible with. We either believe God hates sex and doesn't want us to experience the pleasure, or God doesn't know what He's talking about when He tells us to wait until we are married. Reality check, God loves sex. He invented it and He wants us to have a ton of it! But He wants us to enjoy it in a marriage context because we really have no understanding of the emotional consequences that come with sleeping around with multiple partners. Living in purity now, even though it is extremely tough, is one of the best gifts we can give to the one person we actually want to spend the rest of our life with. God knew what He was doing when He invented sex and He wants us to have the best sex ever, with our spouse. Young people: please do not look for love until you realize how loved you are by a God who calls you His own. You may get a relationship but you won't know how to keep it! True love waits but you don't have to wait to experience true love from God.

The truth is, Satan doesn't want us to realize how scared he is of the power living in us from Christ. I was recently watching a show on lions. I love lions and think they are incredible creatures! What blew me away however, was one of the reasons for why lions roar. Lions often roar to induce fear in prey BEFORE they attack. They creep up close, and then roar before they attack so their prey is struck with a fear that leaves them paralyzed. It is simply a scare tactic. My mind went immediately to 1 Peter 5:8. This Scripture says, "Be alert and of sober mind. Your enemy the devil prowls around like a roaring lion looking for someone to devour." What do you see in this verse that reveals the true nature of Satan? The most important word in 1 Peter 5:8 is the word 'like'. See, Satan is not a lion. He is trying to be a lion, but he is only a little kitty cat. His roar isn't even a roar, rather a simple 'meow'. Satan is panicking, filled with anxiety. As Bishop Jamie Englehart says, "Satan knows at the cross Jesus defanged and declawed him." So, he runs around trying to condemn people into a life away from the grace of God. He's trying to bring anyone he can down with him. Satan's greatest fear is that we will realize our identity as sons and daughters; that God loves us and is proud of us despite our actions. He fears we will understand we are children of God by birth, not by worth. He fears we will find our security in Christ and turn the world upside down for the Gospel. He's busy lying, tempting, disguising, sifting, snatching, blinding, enslaving, and destroying those who don't know their true identity, worth, and value as sons and daughters. Satan has no real power! We have nothing to fear at all. Romans 8:31 says, "If God is for us, who can be against us?"

Satan has no power against those filled with the Spirit. We don't need to get more of the Holy Spirit; the Holy Spirit needs to get more of us. Isn't it interesting how ONLY in the presence of God is surrender the first step to victory? Surrender in our culture is not a good thing. It shows one to be a coward, weak, and pathetic. It shows one has given up and won't continue to fight or strive for the victory. In every context outside of the Gospel, surrender is a sign of defeat. But when we surrender to the will of the Father and allow the truth of the Spirit to fill our lives, God gives us power. His strength overcomes our weaknesses and His grace dominates shame. It's time for us to actually believe God is for us. It's time for us to plow ahead in His strength as we follow His goodness. It's time for us to realize the Spirit is here to convince us of our sonship! It's time for us to surrender to a God who has been obsessed with us since we took our first breath of air! The *"angel of light"* is fallen! His authority in our lives is no more! We are sons and daughters, filled with the Spirit, capable of doing *immeasurably more than all we ask or imagine, according to His power that is at work withIN us*!

CHAPTER 7

GRACE CHANGES EVERYTHING

What is grace? So many people believe grace is a concept. However, grace is not a concept. It's also not an idea, theory, a feel good story, or a get out of jail free card. Grace is a person and His name is Jesus, and when we believe grace to be a person, it changes everything.

As I said in the beginning, I don't like a lot of rules. I assume most of us don't. If you're anything like me, you're the type of person that wants to do the opposite of what you're told to do. For example, do you ever go around touching every wall you see? I hope the answer is 'no', but the moment someone puts up a 'wet paint: do not touch' sign, what do you do? That's right, you touch the wall to see if the paint has dried. I could go on and on with examples of things we do when told not to but the truth is, we don't like to be told 'no'.

Here's the problem with rules: many people think Christianity is all about rules and limitations to 'fun'. However, the Bible is not a rulebook! You've heard the saying that rules are meant to be broken but when it comes to a list of do's and don'ts, most 'rules' really come down to personal conviction. Not everything in the Bible is black and white. In fact, culture constantly changes. What was wrong for your parents might not be wrong for you today and vice versa. However, things get complicated when we make our own convictions the 'mandatory' convictions of all people. This is what the Pharisees were doing when they kept adding laws to reach holiness. But laws and rules only address behavior. The Gospel has nothing to do with behavior; it has everything to do with trusting a Savior who loves us in spite of us. Jesus doesn't want our good deeds, He wants our desires. That is not an external issue; it's a heart issue. We must be careful to not draw arbitrary lines in the ground about what activities are sinful. If the Bible does not condemn it, let moderation rule.

We talked about Karma and the lifestyles of Buddhists and Hindus in Chapter 2. Remember, Karma is the belief that bad things happen to bad people and good things happen to good people. When people do good things to earn something or think God owes them for their obedience, what does that tell you about their love? Do we obey to get something we think we deserve or do we obey simply because God loves us? Sadly, this is how many Christians act. They believe God is upset with them or disappointed in their choices. They feel convicted so they believe they have to do something good to make up for their bad behavior. They feel like they are too bad, dirty, and unworthy or that they need to fix up their life before they walk into a church. But when did God loving you have anything to do with the way you live life? Where do we get this belief that you have to do good things and be a better person before God can save you, redeem you, forgive you, love you, or even have an intimate relationship with you?

The bottom line is, it's impossible to love God when we are unsure about His feelings towards us. Have you ever been in a disastrous relationship? I dated this girl in college way longer than I should have because as an average looking dude, she was way hotter than me. I grew comfortable with her so I ignored all the red flags, which actually caused more harm than good. What I didn't learn until later in life was how needy I was. I thought I was a great guy but I was very insecure; an issue that constantly led me to fish for compliments. I would frequently check in and compare myself with other guys. I would continuously seek affirmation, a love language I didn't know I needed. This is what happens when we try to find our validation in people instead of resting in the unconditional love of God.

I believe we have all had bad relationships; whether it's been with an ex, a parent, a friend, or a boss. Relationships fade and our hearts become scarred. We start to believe God views us in the same light as our earthly relationships. Maybe it was a father that was non-existent, an abusive spouse, a backstabbing friend, or a ministry mentor failing and leaving us brokenhearted. If we are not careful, we will start to view our Heavenly Father through the lens of our broken experiences with people. We believe lies that say God is disappointed in us, upset, or angry at our life choices. We fail to believe that God truly does love us. I mean, how can this be? I constantly fail! Yet, this is what makes God's love so incredible.

Here's a fact: God's not angry with us. He is not looking

down at us in disgust. He is not rattled or surprised when we fail. He is not mad! You may say, dude, I've read stories in the Bible about God opening up the Earth and swallowing up people in their disobedience (Numbers 16) or the countless stories of God being moved to anger during the life of the Israelites. True, God responded with consequences to their actions but only because He was in covenant with them through the Mosaic Law. (The Mosaic Law, also known as the old covenant, are the 10 commandments God gave to Moses on Mount Sinai in Exodus 20 and Deuteronomy 5). Through this covenant, they had curses and blessings due to the system they created. However, this system was never what God wanted. God wanted a direct relationship with them. In fact, if you read the story in Deuteronomy, it was the Israelites that refused to go up the mountain to meet with God because they were afraid. They wanted the system that was created between God and Moses: one that had blessings for obedience and curses for disobedience (Deuteronomy 27-28). So when Christ was crucified, He fulfilled the old covenant or Mosaic Law and brought a new system or new covenant in play through grace and faith in Jesus Christ. And as you read this, you may be thinking to yourself, 'I thought God was the same yesterday, today, and forever? Well, He is (Hebrews 13). Let me explain. Jesus Christ came to Earth and lived the perfect life, then went to Calvary and died for all of our sins: past, present, and future. Did you know that by the blood of Jesus, a new covenant was made instantly? This time however, the covenant wasn't made between God and people but with Jesus and the Father. It's a covenant that can never be changed. A covenant that allows us to stand righteous before God as sons and daughters because of our belief in Jesus. A covenant that God always wanted us to have because it means a direct relationship with Him! A covenant that shows us that Jesus is who God is: a God of love and grace. Jesus reveals the Father as the loving God He has always been. He's under a new covenant with us because of what Jesus did on the cross. This is again why the Stauros is so amazing. Not only did Jesus remove all condemnation on the cross, but He also fully fulfilled the old covenant. The price was huge, but it was paid for in full when Jesus took the nails in our place. And because Jesus took the nails, God is able to look at every one of us in light of Jesus. He's not mad at us, He's mad about us and He wants us to experience this radical love that is not based on how well we perform or how obedient we are. I tend to get more upset at myself than God is. I tend to constantly beat myself up, but in Christ there is no condemnation. The only One perfect enough to condemn us is Jesus, but He doesn't. Instead, He loves us, even when we don't deserve it.

In Luke 19 we see a story of the tax collector named Zacchaeus. In this culture, tax collectors were hated. In the Jewish Misnah, it stated that tax collectors were so despised they weren't even considered people. They were considered animals and you were actually free to lie to tax collectors because lying to an animal was not a sin. This dude was also short. I heard a Pastor say the Greek word used in verse 3 is the word used to describe the body of an undeveloped child. I've researched that out and haven't found that explanation but it's safe to say he was a very small guy. So here is Zacchaeus, extremely short and extremely hated. Jesus comes to town but Zacchaeus can't see over the crowd. He runs ahead and climbs a sycamore-fig tree. In verse 5 it tells us when Jesus reaches the spot, He looks up as if to tell Zacchaeus, *I know who you are and I know where you've been.* Jesus tells him to come down and invites Himself over for a meal. Again, understanding culture is very important because to eat with someone meant you embraced and accepted them. This is why Jesus got so much flak from the Pharisees when He would share meals with prostitutes and sinners. Have you ever noticed that when sinners got around Jesus, they never felt condemned?

So here Jesus is, eating a meal with Zacchaeus. But the conversation, if any, is not recorded in Scripture. We don't know if Jesus tells this man to change or gives a sermon, but we do know that whatever took place changed Zacchaeus' life forever. Zacchaeus stands up and says he will repay anyone he has cheated four times the amount and give half of his possessions to the poor. What?! Notice that Zacchaeus doesn't give because he has to but because he wants to. It's also interesting to note that according to the law, he would have been required to repay 120% back to those he cheated. However, the grace he receives from Jesus he decides to repay 400% back to those he cheated. Grace will always lead us to be more generous than the requirements of the law. Zacchaeus had an experience with a God whose love is unconditional and it radically changed his life forever. Every other religion in the world says we have to change first, then we'll be able to find 'god'. Yet Jesus says His salvation finds us. The entire Gospel message is: God accepts you. He loves you. His grace is sufficient. Once Zacchaeus was accepted, he wanted to change. He wasn't changed by rules or a command. He was changed by a moment with Jesus. We are not transformed by being told what to do for God, but rather by hearing the news about what God has already done for us. When we allow ourselves to have a moment with Jesus, a moment realizing He truly loves us, it changes everything.

This grace God offers is crazy, and yet some people still abuse it. However, as I explained earlier in this chapter, those who abuse grace don't understand that grace is not a concept, theory, feel good story, or a get out of jail free card. Nevertheless, if grace couldn't be abused, it wouldn't be called grace. I've even heard that one needs to balance grace with rules or law. One pastor I heard put that argument to rest when he said, "Grace doesn't need to be balanced, because grace is all there is." Grace truly is amazing, and usually the people who have a problem with grace when it's preached accurately are religious folk. They talk about the dangers of the grace message as if there are no dangers living under performance-based religion. The reason why religious or legalistic people have such a hard time accepting this unadulterated grace is because there is no measuring stick. Our flesh loves to judge, evaluate, control, and manipulate other people all in an effort to feel 'better than' someone else. Besides, it feels good to think we are better than someone because we don't do what they do.

The reality is, some people will abuse grace. People think if we preach grace as accurately as it really is then some will rebel knowing God will forgive them. But that's the problem; because grace is not a proposition, principal, or formula. Grace is a person and His name is Jesus. Those who willingly abuse grace still don't understand it. Grace isn't a do what we want card. It's a do what God wants card. When we grasp this amazing truth, that God will use us in spite of us because He loves us in spite of us, we won't want to do whatever we want. We'll want to do whatever He wants.

I like to read biographies, specifically about pro athletes. I love to see what trials these people have overcome and the adversity they have had to power through. Having a legend for a father who attended Michigan State, my loyalty is to the green and white. Therefore, I despise the University of Michigan. My favorite college football game every year is when MSU and UofScuM play each other for the state bragging rights. The winner of this game receives the Paul Bunyan trophy. Growing up, Paul Bunyan was a tall tale lumberjack figure accompanied by Babe, his blue ox. Then I read about his long lost brother (I think) John Bunyan, the author of *Pilgrim's Progress*. John Bunyan was actually arrested and put in prison for preaching the grace message. His accusers told him, "You can't go on telling people that Christ's righteousness has been credited to them in full. If they believe that, they'll feel like they can do whatever they want." John Bunyan responded, "If people really see that Christ's righteousness has been given to them entirely as a gift, they'll do whatever He wants."[1]

People don't need an excuse to sin, they are going to sin regardless. They need the truth of who Jesus is and how He really sees us. When we sin, we don't fall away from the cross, we fall towards it (Romans 5:20). When we sin, God is not mad or even disappointed. His grace is what is sufficient to lead us to a place where we can rest in His love and forgiveness. Grace does not motivate us to abuse it; it motivates us to realize the righteousness we already have right now because Christ dwells in us!

The point of following Jesus is to keep focusing on His love for us. Spiritual disciplines are great, but the only way to truly grow in our love for God is to stand in awe and grasp how much God sincerely loves us. If God created us, then God essentially created the love we have for Him. This love is what will actually move us into a relationship with God because He loves us in spite of what we do. God's interest in us is not determined by our interest in Him. His love is not determined by our obedience. When we do what is right to feel better about ourselves, we are missing the point of the Gospel. Most of the church world practices 'restraint', rather than manifesting real inward change. I've caught myself saying, "If I wasn't a Christian, I'd knock you out!" But beating people up or being a tough guy is not what I need to define me. If we refrain from "sin" because we know it's wicked we may be concerned with the wrong things. We should refrain from "sin" because we're in love with Jesus. The same thing is true in my marriage. I refrain from having an affair not because it is wrong, but because I am in love with my wife! The Gospel story of grace is what motivates and sustains me regardless of what season I'm walking in.

As I talk with believers, I wonder if our focus is right. We constantly feel like we need to prove our love for God instead of just dwelling on God's love for us. He doesn't love a future you, He loves you as you are right now. In the Gospel of John, we see a dialogue between Peter, John, and Jesus. The writer of John (himself) when talking about himself writes, "the disciple whom Jesus loved." Now that's funny. John seems to be more concerned with Jesus' love for him than his own love for Jesus. In fact, here's a question you may have never asked: why is John the only disciple who is at the foot of the cross when Jesus is crucified? Where are the other disciples? Where is Peter? Jesus spends three years pouring into these guys and the only disciple to show up at His death is John.

In Luke 22:62 after Peter had denied Jesus three times, it says he went outside and wept bitterly. Where is Peter at the cross? He's crying because of what he had done. He's crying because he denied Jesus, and so many of us are just like Peter.

We don't verbally deny Jesus but we deny Him with our lifestyle. Then we come to church on Sunday and emotionally beat ourselves up. We beat ourselves up because we are trying to do better. We think if we try harder we'll get it right, but what we need to grasp is that we simply need to fall in love with a God who is already in love with us.

As I was seeking the answer as to why Peter didn't show up at the cross, the reason hit me while I was listening to a sermon from Pastor Daryl Banet. He said, "If you want to have a pity party, every demon in hell will show up." When I wrote that down, I made the connection as to why Peter never showed up. Peter missed the cross because condemnation showed up through a pity party of shame, and the enemy does the same with us today. However, Jesus turns our shame into a showcase of His grace. Religion tells us we have to work for it; we have to get right with God daily, weekly, and monthly. Religion says we need to keep marching, keep trying, get better, and stay better. But God does something that changes the game for Christians forever. So many people today don't get involved in the church, don't serve, and don't give where there are needs because they feel like they aren't good enough. Or maybe they get stuck having a pity party by themselves in condemnation and shame apart from the grace of the cross, just like Peter. God is not angry, God is love! As Andrew Farley says, "In the work of the Son, we see the heart of a Father who accepts us with no strings attached."[2] His affection toward us is stronger than we can possibly imagine. Now we get to be a part of God's plan! God's love is expressed through Jesus because He did what we couldn't do for ourselves. The cross represents the ultimate sacrifice, the ultimate picture of love.

In some Christian circles, you hear sermons preached

that when Jesus was crucified, God actually turned His back on Him. They say that because God can't look at sin...apparently. Those who say God can't look at sin reference the Bible. But there is only one verse that remotely talks about that. It's found in Habakkuk 1:13 which says, "Your eyes are too pure to look on evil; you cannot tolerate wrongdoing...." But the verse continues, "...Why then do you tolerate the treacherous? Why are you silent while the wicked swallow up those more righteous than themselves?" Or in other words, God you're too pure to look at sin but then why do you look? There is not one verse in the rest of Scripture mentioning anything about God being too holy to not see evil as it happens. If that were the case, we'd all be screwed. In Matthew 27:46, we read what Jesus said on the cross, "My God, my God, why have you forsaken me?" It's quite easy to believe that God forsook Jesus on the cross but that is not what happened here. God never turned His back on His beloved!

I believe that because of Jesus' circumstances and becoming sin (2 Corinthians 5:21), for the first time in His life He could not sense the relationship of the Father. In His pain, both physically and spiritually, He cried out. In His humanity, Jesus felt disconnected as if God had turned His back on Him but God never once forsook His Son. I believe Jesus actually understands and sympathizes with us when we feel this way. Recently, I was at a conference when Bishop Jamie Englehart and Dr. Jonathan Welton shared even more insight into this subject. In fact, turn to Matthew 27:46 right now to see what happened on the cross during this moment. You will see a little letter after the verse (in the NIV it is the letter 'c'). At the bottom of the page it highlights Psalm 22:1. The Psalms are actually songs. In this culture, most Jews would have sung the songs of Psalms regularly and most of them would have been memorized. So when Jesus quotes Psalm 22, which starts with, "My God, My God, why have you forsaken me," the Jews would have remembered this Psalm and they would have sung it. Was Jesus singing on the cross? I don't know, but He at least started it. In fact, the Jews would have continued with the entire Psalm and everyone around them would have understood exactly what was now happening; that Jesus really was the Messiah and that He was fulfilling the Mosaic covenant. Read the entire Psalm, it's amazing. I've included verses 14-18, 24, 31.

14 I am poured out like water,
And all my bones are out of joint.
My heart has turned to wax;
It has melted within me.
15 My mouth is dried up like a potsherd,
And my tongue sticks to the roof of my mouth;
You lay me in the dust of death.
16 Dogs surround me,
a pack of villains encircles me;
they pierce my hands and my feet.
17 All my bones are on display;
people stare and gloat over me.
18 They divide my clothes among them
and cast lots for my garment.

24 For he has not despised or scorned
the suffering of the afflicted one;
he has not hidden his face from him
but has listened to his cry for help

31 They will proclaim his righteousness,

declaring to a people yet unborn:
He has done it!

Those in attendance would have sung those words, revealing the reality of what was taking place before them. Psalm 22:24 clearly states that God never hid His face from Jesus but listened to his cry for help. This may also be the reason why the centurions and the men casting lots for His clothes exclaimed in Matthew 27:54, "Surely He was the Son of God!" You would too if they started singing that *His clothes would be divided and they would cast lots for His garments* as you had just casted lots for His garments! The best part about this Psalm is the last verse, which proclaims His righteousness as He says, "He has done it!" Or, "It is finished!" Jesus finished what we could never do so we could have a direct relationship with the Father, something old covenant believers never had.

Here is the truth that we need to constantly remind ourselves of: God never forsakes us! He is with us always, just like He was always with Jesus. Just like in the garden when Adam and Eve sinned and they ran away from God. It wasn't God who turned His back on them. It was God who pursued them and it's God who is constantly pursuing us. Whether we feel it or not, God has never left our side, nor will He ever leave us. We can run but God will never stop running after us. Are you tired from running? Are you tired of trying to be better and work harder? We can play games and think other people are blessed because they are 'good' or we can realize it's not about our strength, or discipline, or love for God. It is all about His incredible love for us! Maybe it's time for you to stop running and fall into the loving arms of a God who will never drop you.

CHAPTER 8

WEAPONS OF MASS DISTRACTION

Violence is everywhere. No matter where you turn, how much you hate it, or what you do to prevent it, it constantly seems to be right around the corner. With violence comes hate and evil. As long as Satan is alive, hate, violence, and evil will continue to exist. Many people struggle with this reality. They ask questions such as, 'If God is in control, why does so much evil exist?' 'How can a loving God exist when there is so much hatred, violence, and crime?' 'Why didn't God just start over when Adam and Eve sinned and brought death into the world?' We could go on and on about why 'bad' things seem to happen to 'good' people while 'evil' people seem to flourish. I mean, come on God – don't you care about all these horrible things happening on your Earth?!

When tragedy happens, it more likely than not forces people to run toward God. Truth is, evil things happen. But to claim God doesn't exist because there is evil does not solve the problem of evil. Many people refuse to believe in God because of the unjust suffering happening throughout the world. They wonder how God can allow this insanity. We know evil when we see it but we don't know how to identify it before it happens. Also, just because one may abandon belief in God doesn't make the problem of evil go away. To me, evil actually proves God does exist. If we don't know what hate is, do we really know love? If we don't know what bad is, do we really know good? If we don't partake in the sufferings of Christ, can we really identify with Him? As we talked about in Chapter 6, according to Ephesians 6, all of us are in some kind of spiritual war. There is nothing Satan wants more than to have us blame God and run from Him because of the evil choices of human beings.

Let's face it, God gets a bad rep and blamed for things He doesn't do. Is God really in control like we say He is? Does He actually control my decisions? Is He the puppet master in the sky, forcing me to fall in love with Him? Or in His sovereignty, does He give us free will to make decisions on our own: decisions to follow or deny Him, to do good or to do evil? I mean, kids go to school with weapons and injure or kill unsuspecting students and God gets blamed for it, yet God has continually been removed from every aspect of the educational process until bad things happen. And explain to me again why it is okay to pray during school violence yet not okay and intolerant to bring up God in any other context related to education? Say a marriage is falling apart or your kids seem to be making terrible life choices and again, God gets the blame. Someone is thousands of dollars in debt, which may be the reason for why the marriage is falling apart, and one more time God gets the blame; yet as Dave Ramsey says, "It was you buying things you don't need with money you don't have to impress people you don't like."[1] Or we don't get the dream job and maybe someone else gets the promotion we thought we deserved and God gets the blame again. But maybe we didn't prepare ourselves properly for the opportunity or maybe God is asking us to trust Him because the perfect job is about to become available or doesn't even exist yet. For students, maybe you didn't get accepted to the college you wanted to attend, that girl breaks up with you, or you get cut from the sports team or choir you wanted to be a part of and God continues to get blamed for it; but maybe He has different plans for your life. We continue to walk by faith in life and we try to love people like God has loved us but then the unthinkable happens and we experience betrayal in a friendship or death of a loved one. Then, we turn our anger towards God when it is actually Satan who is the author of betrayal and death!

So, is God in control like we think He is? I think a better understanding of God and Satan will help us answer these questions. First, yes, God is sovereign but He gets blamed way too much for things that are credited to Satan. I've heard the answer to this question best explained as a property owner. God is sovereign over the property but He does not control everything that happens on the property. God is not a control freak. He doesn't make us do anything, He only invites us to be a part of His plan and leads us to do His will. He does not possess people; He fills them with His Spirit. It is Satan who possesses and destroys. As a believer, I have surrendered my life to God and given Him the authority to lead me by His Spirit because without God, I can do nothing. However, without mankind, God chooses to do nothing. This puts a large responsibility on people to bring the goodness of God to everyone, not to earn favor from God, but because we understand that we already have His favor! Therefore, we need to stop blaming God for everything that happens. He gives us the choice to make a difference in this world for His glory. Romans 8:28 is clear about this when it states that all things work together for good for those who love God. Notice that it does not say all things are good because not all things that happen in life are good! Yet, God will use all things for His good and perfect will. Second, God doesn't kill anyone. I've heard it too many times at funerals that God has taken so and so 'home'. God doesn't take anyone 'home'. He only receives people. As we talked about in Chapter 6, the Bible tells us that Satan enslaves (2 Timothy 2) and destroys (1 Peter 5). He is the author of destruction but it is Christ who has come to give us life and life to the fullest. Cancer, disease, evil, death, violence, crime, and hate are not from God. Those are all Satan's tools to distract us from the reality that God is love and only gives life. We need to stop blaming the only One Who can actually help us and give us hope, joy, love, and peace among life's greatest hurts.

Another hot question because sin, evil, and death exist, is why didn't God just start over after Adam and Eve sinned? The answer is actually fascinating when we understand that God did. There are many things that God can't actually do. For example, God cannot sin. God cannot tell a lie. God also cannot go against His own word. So, when God gave dominion over to mankind (a body with a soul and spirit) according to Psalm 72, He couldn't go against His word. Therefore, in order for God to start over, He had to get a body. Enter Jesus! Jesus took on flesh, walked the Earth without sin, and existed at this moment as the only person to have the Holy Spirit dwelling inside of Him. Follow me here:

at this point, no one prior to the death of Jesus ever had the Spirit of God dwelling inside of them. The Spirit only came ON people and guided them, never filling them from within. This is why Jesus had to become flesh. He had to remove the veil of our sinful nature so the Holy Spirit could come and dwell within us. God sent Jesus out of Heaven to walk the Earth, to live the perfect life, to die a painful death, and rise three days later so the Spirit of God could live inside of us. God, through the body of Christ, gave Himself back the dominion over mankind. God started over with Jesus, the second Adam! Therefore, there are only two kinds of men on this Earth. Men after the first Adam – fallen and sinful at the core…and men after the second Adam (Jesus) – rescued and forgiven, filled with the love and grace of our Heavenly Father. As Tullian Tchividjian tweeted, "God is not a God of second chances. He's a God of one chance and a second Adam."[2] This second Adam is Jesus and He is amazing!

All in all, suffering and painful experiences throughout life is a given whether you believe in God or not. John 16:20 gives us two promises: you will be sorrowful, but your sorrow will turn to joy. Pain is a guarantee, but joy will always follow pain…eventually. Belief in God does not take away the excruciating circumstances life throws us but it does provide a way to face them when they occur. God gives one hope, courage, and peace to endure because Jesus already experienced suffering and pain like none of us ever will when He paid our penalty on the cross. Timothy Keller puts it this way, "God takes our misery and suffering so seriously that He was willing to take it on Himself…if we embrace the Christian teaching that Jesus is God and that He went to the Cross, then we have deep consolation and strength to face the brutal realities of life on Earth. We can know that God is truly Immanuel - God with us - even in our worst sufferings."[3] Life doesn't always make sense but we can have peace in knowing God is with us through it all. When life gets turned upside down and we don't know why, hold on to the promises of God! In this world, we will have trouble but take heart because Jesus has overcome the world (John 16:33)!

In our culture today, we aren't under attack from weapons of mass destruction; we are under attack from weapons of mass distraction! We are so easily distracted that we focus our energy on things that keep us from being aware of the presence of God on a regular basis. Evil, pain, hate, death, sin, violence all exist, but if we focus so much on the questions as to why, it will distract us from falling in love with a God who is so in love with us; a God who grieves along with us through the hurt; a God who cares about our daily lives and whose grace is sufficient; a God who gets blamed for what Satan does. What would life look like if we were able to remove the distractions that keep us from being 'wowed' by the love of our incredible Father in Heaven? Brady Boyd says, "If there is one thing that keeps otherwise good people from living as selfless carriers of grace, it's that we're too tangled up in the cords of this world to focus our attention on God. We don't see the needs he sees. We don't hear the cries he hears. We don't taste the suffering of so many people in our own backyard who need help."[4]

One of the main areas of distraction for Americans today is wealth. Now don't get me wrong. Money is not bad nor is it bad to want to make a lot of it. In fact, I encourage you to make that paper boo-boo. However, when we love money and the process of making it more than God, that's when it becomes a distraction. But this distraction of wealth is not a new thing. Revelation 3 talks about a specific church in the city of Laodicea. What I'm about to explain is something I learned from Ray Vander Laan who has been teaching Jewish culture using the methods of Jewish education for over 35 years. He explains Revelation 3:15-16 (I know your deeds, that you are neither cold nor hot. I wish you were either one or the other! So, because you are lukewarm – neither hot nor cold – I am about to spit you out of my mouth) in context. First off, the audience in this passage are Christians – believers in the church in Laodicea. This city was in between two cities – Hierapolis (known for its healing hot springs) and Colosse (known for its refreshing cold springs). Laodicea, the richest and most powerful of the three cities, attracted its population because of the opportunity to gain wealth. However, there was a problem. Laodicea was a city built where the hot springs of Hierapolis and the cold springs of Colosse met producing a lukewarm river. This water was not useful for bathing or healing nor was it useful for drinking because it would make people sick. The imagery used in this passage of being hot or cold is important because either you are going to bring healing and comfort to people like the hot spring, or you are going to refresh and encourage people like the cold spring. Instead, you are lukewarm – you don't bring anything good to the table and you make people sick. The challenge here is for Christians to not be distracted by the things of this world but to be hot and cold in our daily lives – to be a people that bring life, healing, restoration, grace, love, and peace that only Jesus can offer. We must be carriers of the encouraging touch of Jesus Christ.

We are distracted a lot! It's hard to see the work of God when our focus is on the negative things going on in and around our lives. For example, I find it humorous whenever I hear people tell me they don't want to go to church or left the church because they claim there are too many hypocrites in the church. Well DUH! Of course there are hypocrites in the church! We all are hypocrites in different areas and circumstances throughout our lives. God knows we are going to fail Him and yet He loves us anyway. However, not going to church because of the hypocrites that exist in every church is like not going on an all-paid for, all-inclusive trip to Aruba because you heard some of the hotel staff were jerks. See, grace is way more amazing than you think it is because God enables us to love all people even though we have skeletons in our closet. Despite our failures, weaknesses, and struggles, God wants us! It's time we put down our weapons of mass distraction!

The comforting reality for me is that we constantly see people in the Bible being distracted by things that aren't really that important. In Luke 10:38-42 we read a story about two sisters: Martha and Mary. Now to be fair, Martha owns the home that this story takes place in while her younger sister, Mary, was being a freeloader! As the homeowner, there comes the responsibility to be hospitable, yet there is a solid principle to be grasped from this story. In fact, Luke tells us that Martha was distracted by the preparations. This word in the Greek literally means to be greatly troubled. Martha is running around trying to make everything perfect, and where is Mary? She's at the feet of Jesus listening to Him teach. Here is Martha, greatly troubled by the stress of being hospitable and even though her intentions are good, she misses Jesus. I don't know about you but I find myself to be a lot like Martha. I constantly have to remind myself to slow down in life and focus in on Jesus, even though I am busy with ministry! When I was first starting off in ministry, someone gave me this word of encouragement: Never get so busy working FOR God that you forget to spend time WITH Him. How many of us are so busy in life that we miss Jesus on a daily basis? My friend Eric Timm says it this way in his book *Static Jedi*, "What happens when we don't get to know God? The same thing that happens in relationships that don't include some measure of continual pursuit."[5]

The most challenging part of this story however, comes in the form of a question from Martha to Jesus. In the craziness of the moment, Martha cries out in her frustration something a lot of us say when we are distracted, depressed, or in need in life. She rushes into the room, sees Mary at His feet, and in a panic she says, "Lord, don't you care?" You know what's interesting about that question? The disciples said the same thing to Jesus when they woke Him up out of their fear and distress according to Mark 4:38 while Jesus was sleeping through the storm. LORD, DON'T YOU CARE?! Your life seems to be falling apart while everyone else around you seems to be thriving and you cry out to God, don't you care?! God, don't you care about my situation? Are you ever going to answer my prayers? Am I ever going to get a break in life?!

The beautiful thing about Jesus is He responds, and in His response His everlasting peace comes upon us! Jesus says to Martha, "You are worried and upset about many things but only one thing is needed" – ME. Christianity does not start with serving Jesus! It starts with Jesus serving us. Right here, in these five verses in Luke 10, we see a picture of grace. Martha focuses on doing many things to receive love from Jesus while Mary focuses on one thing - Jesus' love for her. All throughout Scripture, Jesus is trying to show us that it's not about performing better or trying harder or even about becoming spiritually disciplined (although spiritual disciplines are great). It's all about focusing on the one thing, the only thing that can rescue you – Jesus Christ and His love for people. Nothing will satisfy you like Jesus. Not sex, not the party scene, not money, not the dream job, house, car, or relationships. Nothing satisfies the soul like the love of Christ. Yet, so many of us are running around trying to find satisfaction in unfulfilling idols. Then we get mad at God when things don't go our way and we say exactly what Martha said, "God, don't you care?"

God cares, but we have become so distracted by the world that we forget the one thing, the only thing that matters! When we put our hope in materialistic things, we end up distracted. When we put our hope in people, we end up disappointed. When we put our hope in ourselves, we end up devastated. Yet when we put our hope in Jesus, we end up delivered. When our hope is in anything but Jesus, we will always find ourselves empty.

God's timing is perfect, but when we are hit in the face with a crisis it can seem like it's out of whack! Martha is distracted in Mark 10 but there is another story in Scripture with Martha and Mary found in John 11 that is very similar. Instead of being distracted by house preparations, Martha is distracted by the death of her brother Lazarus. Lazarus is sick and on his deathbed when Martha and Mary send word to Jesus saying, "Lord, the one you love (Lazarus) is sick." (Notice it wasn't about Lazarus' love for Jesus, it was about Jesus' love for Lazarus). Jesus tells them that this sickness will not end in death, yet He stays in the place where He was for two more days. Finally, Jesus arrives only to find out that Lazarus has been dead in the tomb for four days! Think about this from Martha's perspective. In her terrible circumstances, she runs to Jesus knowing He has the power to heal her sick brother. Jesus tells her that Lazarus will not die but then decides to take His sweet time in arriving to his deathbed. So much time that Lazarus has been buried for four days! Can you imagine the distress Martha must have felt during those four days? Those four days must have felt like months! Not only is she grieving the loss of her brother but she must have been ticked off at Jesus. All this time she has believed Him to be the Messiah. He also promised her that Lazarus' sickness would not end in death, and now she is faced with the thought that Jesus lied to her. She cries out to Jesus telling Him that if only He would have been there, her brother would not have died. The interesting thing about this phrase is that Martha says it in verse 21, almost in an accusing tone, while Mary says the exact same thing later in verse 32, yet her tone was different. In fact, the passage states that Mary fell at Jesus' feet. Notice the difference in posture because posture is important! The Scriptures then tell us that when Jesus sees Mary crying that He too weeps along with her. Why? Because Jesus mourns with those who mourn.

Jesus, in His empathy, has the people there remove the gravestone and tells Lazarus to walk out of the tomb. Lazarus, after being dead for four days, comes walking out of the tomb still wrapped in the grave clothes. One of the greatest miracles ever recorded is also one of the most frustrating stories in the Bible because of our mindset and understanding of time here on Earth. What was devastating to Martha because of her perspective was actually one of the greatest gifts to us who read the story because God is not limited by time. I mean, there have been countless times in my life that I have been frustrated with God because I thought my prayers went unanswered. My perspective was simply that of being distracted by living in the moment of, "I need what I want right now". What I perceive as unanswered prayers are simply just delays. What you are asking God for in this moment might be delayed until you can properly steward what it is you are seeking. You might be delayed but you are not defeated. God is always on time, but He is not on a timer. Be still and know that He is God! Hope in Christ brings us confidence, assurance, and peace.

Have you ever noticed how God seems to answer our prayers with this confidence, assurance, and peace that only He can provide? Let me blow your mind for a minute with something that God has been blowing my mind with lately. 1 Thessalonians 5:17 tells us that we are to "pray without ceasing". I used to be so frustrated with that verse because how in the world am I able to pray without ever stopping? I mean, come on God…I've got stuff to do and so do you! We have school, homework, sports, work, jobs, family, hobbies, etc., the list goes on. How can anyone pray without ceasing?! That phrase "pray without ceasing" in the Greek can mean, "come to rest". This is where this verse changed the game for me. Matthew 11:28 says, "Come to me, all who are weary and burdened, and I will give you rest." That word rest (eirene) in the Greek is the equivalent Hebrew word for peace (shalom). Rest has little to do with the absence of pain or conflict but it has everything to do with the peace that only God gives in the midst of a daily struggle. Rest means security, completion, and peace! The most important thing that believers can do is believe God to be who He says He is. In that belief, God gives us the peace that surpasses all understanding (Philippians 4). See, to pray without ceasing is all about resting in knowing who our Father is. It's not about countless hours of praying. Smith Wigglesworth is quoted as saying, "I don't often spend more than half an hour in prayer, but I never go more than half an hour without praying."[6] Communicating with God is not something that is measured in minutes, rather it is a lifestyle.

Spending time with God isn't just limited to reading our Bible, praying, and going to church. Do we realize that when we are resting in the finished work of Jesus that we are spending time with Him? That when we believe God to be who He says He is and trust Him, with not only our life but with our needs that we are spending time with Him? That when we keep our relationships pure that we are spending time with Him? That when we're hanging out with our friends without compromising Scripture that we are actually spending time with Jesus? That when we love our spouse well that we're spending time with Him? That when we invest in the next generation that we're spending time with Him? The reality is, we spend a lot more time with Jesus than we even know. We just need to change our perspectives and the way we think. We need to rest in the love that God has for us and we need to be confident in our position as sons and daughters. It's time for us to put down the weapons of mass distraction!

CHAPTER 9

CANNIBALISM

When you think of the word cannibalism, what is the first thing that comes to mind? You might be the kind of person that thinks of the definition, which leads to your stomach turning over. Or you think of the academy award-winning actor Anthony Hopkins and the character he played in Hannibal Lector. Either way, cannibalism is one of the creepiest words in the English dictionary. It can be hard for us in American culture to understand that some societies in different parts of the world actually practice this kind of stuff. However, in the animal kingdom, it's a bit more common than we may know. Female spiders (which I believe came from the fall), such as the Australian Redback and the Black Widow, tend to murder and eat the male spider after mating. I don't know if Iggy Azalea is a cannibal or not but apparently she loves like a Black Widow, baby. If you're totally lost as to who Iggy is just ask your kids, they listen to her. The male Golden Crab spider from Canada however, is a little smarter than the Australian Redback and the Black Widow. In fact, he uses his spider silk not to spin webs but to restrain the female during mating so that she doesn't kill him. I think our marriages can learn a lot from the Golden Crab spider (kidding, unless you're into that stuff). Did you know the female Praying Mantis are also known for ripping off the males head after mating? Why is it that all these females have so much aggression come mating season? If you don't know why that's funny it's because you're single. Also on this list of cannibals are Sand Tiger sharks, Scorpions, Hamsters, and Rattlesnakes. If you really want to be disgusted, go research the Parasitic Wasp. I did so and totally lost my appetite. Cannibalism to say the least is jacked up!

As I think about this process of 'eating your own', it seems as though many Christians are more like cannibals than we would like to admit. Believers are called to live a life that sets them apart from the world. They are called to model a standard; a standard they themselves will never be able to fully uphold, and a standard that causes our hypocritical actions. So what happens when we as believers don't model the standard we are supposed to be living by? The answer to that question is easy: we condemn them. The grace that we have been offered by God every day is the same grace we are supposed to offer to other people on the daily…yet we don't. Let's just call a spade a spade. No one is perfect. In fact, I'm pretty jacked up and you'd be shocked to know that as a pastor, I think of some pretty ridiculously sinful stuff. But this is why I love Jesus and need Him! What we don't do a good job of preaching in American churches today, is that the grace God uses to reach people who do not know Him, is the same grace He offers to everyone every day. We need grace every day because it's His grace that is sufficient. As Ephesians 2:8-9 says, "For it is by grace you have been saved, through faith – and this is not from yourselves, it is the gift of God – not by works, so that no one can boast." God's grace is way better than we think it is.

What's even worse than condemning other believers is the fact that we condemn people who oppose what we believe. We are to model the standard, not rebuke those who don't. If we aren't careful, we can become arrogant and prideful without realizing that Jesus also died for the person we look down on the most. The reality is, we will never be able to reach the people we picket. Christians love to be known for what they are against. They love to tell people they are wrong instead of showing the love and grace of Christ. If we want to reach people that have different views and beliefs, we are going to have to learn how to love and accept others through our disagreements. Last time I checked, there was not one time in the life of Jesus that when He got around a bunch of prostitutes, tax collectors, and sinners that those people ever felt condemned. So, if sinners were attracted to Jesus because He loved them without condemnation, shouldn't sinners be attracted to our churches? Gregory Boyd says, "Perhaps the greatest indictment on evangelical churches today is that they are not generally known as refuge houses for sinners – places where hurting, wounded, sinful people can run and find a love that does not question, an understanding that does not judge, and an acceptance that knows no conditions."[1] It's time for God's people to love like Jesus loves.

What I want to focus on and challenge you with in this chapter is to be less critical of others, regardless if they believe things differently than you. There's a lot of theology out there that differs from each other but as long as Jesus stays the main thing, why do Christians who wear the same jersey, feel the need to always bash each other? We're supposedly on the same team!!! The crazy thing is, with just the above sentences, you probably already have someone in mind as to why it is okay for you to analyze and evaluate some prosperity gospel preacher or mega church pastor. Besides, you watched the five-minute YouTube clip and totally know the context or the behind the scenes as to what that person is going through. Gregory Boyd says, "In the name of correct biblical doctrine, Christians have frequently destroyed the unity of the body of Christ, refusing to minister or worship together because of doctrinal differences, sometimes viciously attacking those who disagree with them...People who get life from religion need to be right and need to try to make other people right or expose them for being wrong."[2] When we try to hold people accountable yet do not have a voice in their life, it actually causes more problems. This is why Jesus says to have these conversations in private...meaning there must be some kind of relationship involved!

The other excuse as to why people publicly bash other believers is because we claim we need to warn people of false teachers. They bring up Matthew 7, 2 Timothy 4, and 2 Peter 2, but understanding context is so important. Matthew 7 talks about being aware of false prophets who appear in sheep clothes but inwardly are ravenous wolves. It tells us that we will know them by their fruits. 2 Timothy 4 talks about people not wanting sound doctrine but will be looking to have their ears tickled. 2 Peter 2 talks about false prophets and teachers rising up among us bringing destructive heresies, the truth will be blasphemed, their greed will exploit you, and their condemnation is not idle. All of these passages of Scripture when talking about false teachers are actually warning us against those that teach condemnation, guilt, shame, and any other non-grace message of the goodness and love of Jesus. Guilt driven messages are great for short-term statistics of behavior modification that never breed real change and growth. This is why many Christians still struggle with the same things because they try so hard on their own to please a God that they've failed to realize is already pleased with them. Not because of their actions but because of their belief in Him! It's tiring trying to gain the attention and approval of Jesus through your behavior, which is why many people give up on Jesus. They give up because they don't realize they already have the full attention and approval of a God who is scandalously in love with them in spite of their actions. If we're honest, we like behavior modification messages or "having our ears tickled" because we believe that grace really isn't that easy or amazing. We like to check things off our list of behaviors we must partake in because it gives us a measuring stick of how well we are doing spiritually. Yet this is not how God operates. Again, any message that breeds condemnation, guilt, or shame is not from God. God loves people! That is why He sent His Son – to rescue us from our own condemnation and set us free (Romans 8:1. John 3:18.).

Criticism, negative opinions, and the need to publicly speak ill of people regardless if what you're saying is right, is the reason why many people don't want what our churches have to offer. Don't get me wrong; there is a place to challenge and correct brothers and sisters who preach inaccurately or don't leave a great example of following Christ. But to say things on blogs, social media, or in our pulpits is not the place for it. Besides, the pulpits should only be used to talk about Jesus! There are far too many people bashing other believers without knowing what they know and walking where they've walked. We have a lot of opinions and form these judgments on leaders that we don't personally know. Then we unfairly put them down without them having a chance of a rebuttal. We as Christians, and notice I include myself because I am just as guilty, tend to eat our own. This should not be. As Brady Boyd says, "Among themselves, the Pharisees were a loving, generous, compassionate people. But for people outside that inner circle, the reception was icy cold. When I look at churches today, I see that not much has changed. We say we are kind and caring and focused on freeing people in Jesus' name. But as soon as one from our fellowship falls, we quietly usher him or her out the back door."[3]

Michael Cheshire, an author who writes in the Leadership Journal for Christianity Today, wrote a blog in 2012 titled, *"Going To Hell with Ted Haggard – What I learned about grace and redemption through my friendship with a Christian pariah."* If you've been in church culture long enough, you know Ted Haggard. Unfortunately, you probably know him for what he did to cause a church split rather than for what he is doing right now to advance the Kingdom of God. Currently, he's ministering to broken people who drastically need hope...hope that only Jesus provides daily to broken people. After the first time I read the blog, I remember weeping bitterly at the reality of how critical I had become with fellow brothers and sisters in Christ. How desperately we need the grace of God in our own lives and how important it is to extend that grace to all people. Cheshire explains his encounter with the reality of just how much Christians tend to eat their own...

I didn't plan to care about Ted Haggard. After all, I have access to Google and a Bible. I heard about what he did and knew it was wrong. I saw the clips from the news and the HBO documentary about his life after his fall. I honestly felt bad for him but figured it was his own undoing. When the topic came up with others I know in ministry, we would feign sadness, but inside we couldn't care less. One close friend said he would understand it more if Ted had just sinned with a woman. I agreed with him at the time. It's amazing how much more mercy I give to people who struggle with sins I understand. The further their sin is from my own personal struggles, the more judgmental and callous I become. I'm not proud of that. It's just where I was at that time in my walk. But that all changed in one short afternoon.

A while back I was having a business lunch at a sports bar in the Denver area with a close atheist friend. He's a great guy and a very deep thinker. During lunch, he pointed at the large TV screen on the wall. It was set to a channel recapping Ted's fall. He pointed his finger at the HD and said, "That is the reason I will not become a Christian. Many of the things you say make sense, Mike, but that's what keeps me away." It was well after the story had died down, so I had to study the screen to see what my friend was talking about. I assumed he was referring to Ted's hypocrisy. "Hey man, not all of us do things like that," I responded. He laughed and said, "Michael, you just proved my point. See, that guy said sorry a long time ago. Even his wife and kids stayed and forgave him, but all you Christians still seem to hate him. You guys can't forgive him and let him back into your good graces. Every time you talk to me about God, you explain that he will take me as I am. You say he forgives all my failures and will restore my hope, and as long as I stay outside the church, you say God wants to forgive me. But that guy failed while he was one of you, and most of you are still vicious to him." Then he uttered words that left me reeling: "You Christians eat your own. Always have. Always will." ... When Ted crawled off that altar and into the arms of a forgiving God, we chose to kill him with our disdain. My concept of grace needed to mature, to grow muscles, teeth, and bad breath. It needed to carry a shield, and most of all, it needed to find its voice... Of course, I understand that if a person doesn't repent there is not a whole lot you can offer. But Ted resigned, confessed, repented, and submitted. He jumped through our many hoops. When will we be cool with him again? When will the church allow God to use him again? It's funny that we believe we get to make that decision.[4]

Wow, it gets me every time. It gets me because I'm guilty of Christian cannibalism too. Cheshire goes on to explain how that encounter changed his heart and how he actually developed a friendship with Ted Haggard as they do ministry in cities not too far apart. What a great story of love and grace. But why do most of us today think that we can determine who should receive this love and grace?

Cannibalism is a disease that tends to grow in our hearts when we see other people succeed or fail. They succeed so we jealously bash them. They fail so we crucify them. Either way, we tend to 'eat our own'.

A couple years ago, Pastor Mark Driscoll was all over the news with controversy as he stepped down as the pastor of Mars Hill Church in Seattle, Washington. Whether you like him or not, you may have read some of the reports found on the internet and have formed some kind of opinion about him. Regardless, he was scheduled to preach for Pastor Robert Morris at Gateway Church during their fall conference before he resigned. Instead of preaching, he simply attended; but what I want to talk about is what Pastor Robert said during the conference about Pastor Mark. He said, "We could crucify him but since someone's already been crucified for him...we could restore him with a spirit of gentleness. It's very sad that in the church, we're the only army that shoots at our wounded." Unfortunately, this is so true. We offer grace to those outside the church but if one of our own falls, we kick them to the curb. This hypocrisy is doing more harm than good. We must offer the kind of grace and love that the Scriptures so frequently talk about. We need to constantly remind ourselves of the grace that God offers us on a daily basis. Let's not be so quick to point out the speck of sawdust in the shortcomings of others while the log in our own life continues to grow like Pinocchio's nose. As Jesus says in Luke 5, "It is not the healthy who need a doctor, but the sick."

As I'm writing this, I just received a text message from a friend who was getting made fun of for attending our church. They said we're too charismatic, yet I know they have never walked through the doors of our church. By definition, charismatic means, "to be compelling attractiveness or charm that can inspire devotion in others." The English word for charismatic comes from the Greek term charisma, which means "gift of grace". So yeah, by those definitions who wouldn't want to inspire others through the gift of grace that we have been given through Jesus Christ. The grace that puts all of us on the same playing field despite our differences, beliefs, mistakes, choices, or failures. The worst part about it is the people making fun of her are Bible believing Christians! They even brought up the fact that I drive a Lexus and therefore am Satan because I own something nice. Not to mention that the Lexus is a 2002 with six figure miles that I bought with cash (Dave Ramsey would be proud). It's almost comical when you are able to see how Satan works even among brothers and sisters in Christ. Satan wants to disrupt the unity of the Gospel. He wants us to have negative feelings towards other believers. He wants us to destroy each other so that we are distracted from reaching more people in need of the good news of what Jesus has done.

This comparison thing we do is eroding us from the inside out. Satan wants us to compare our blessings, knowledge, 'good' deeds, and materialistic things so we become ungrateful and judgmental. Galatians tells us not to compare ourselves with others. It wouldn't tell us that if we all didn't do it at some point in our lives. Can you imagine how happy you would be if you didn't have information about your neighbors and friends to compare yourself with? Comparison only keeps us from enjoying our calling. It kills our joy, robs our blessings, and gives birth to a spirit of entitlement. The same spirit of entitlement that exists in our churches today. The spirit that says that God owes me something because I am 'good', serve, and give. This spirit is a form of religion: a religion that provides us a system of measurement and a false sense of security and comfort in what we have or have not done instead of resting in the finished work of Christ. This spirit says my performance is more significant than what Jesus did on the cross. This spirit is the one that the older brother possessed in the parable of the prodigal son.

Luke 15 is a famous passage about the prodigal son. As I explained in Chapter 4, most sermons tend to focus on the younger son, the son that left and squandered his wealth with prostitutes. Yet it was the older son who had a spirit of entitlement because of his 'good behavior', which caused him to miss the blessings of being a son! He was oblivious to the fact that everything the father had was already his. Both sons were in the wrong: the younger through his actions and the older through his pride. But here is what many people miss about the younger son. It tells us in verse 17, after he had squandered all his wealth, that he came to his senses! If he came to his senses, it must mean he realized he was being an idiot. Sometimes we suffer and there is no explanation as to why we went through what we went through, but most times we suffer because we make stupid choices. What we need to understand is this younger son did not lose his sonship! He lost his senses! We think we can work for or earn God's favor but God calls that pride. Just because we do something bad does not mean we are kicked out of the family. By our belief in Jesus, we become a child of the King. We are not a child by our worth, we are a child by birth! What you may need to do right now in this moment is come back to your senses and realize that you're home as a child in the Kingdom of God. God welcomes you back with the love of a Father who has never crossed his arms at you. You won't find true love in traditions of religious duties. You will only find it in Jesus. He loves you and He wants to celebrate life with you daily! Notice the younger son thought his 'party' days were over when he repented, but the real party was just about to begin!

CHAPTER 10

TOUGH MUDDER

I believe fitness is extremely important to both our physical and spiritual health. The more I work out, the better I feel physically and emotionally. However, I don't really enjoy the process of what it takes to stay fit. Cutting out junk food and working out are things I have to continually train myself to do. So, five to six times a week, I participate in workouts with my pastor such as p90x, Insanity, Crossfit, and weight training. There are a couple people in our church that are fitness gurus who always pressure me to do a Tough Mudder with them. If you don't know what a Tough Mudder is, let me explain. It's an obstacle course that is the king of all obstacle courses. Designed and created by British Special Forces, it's an endurance event where participants attempt to run 10-12 miles while completing 15-20 different military style obstacles along the way. These obstacles include tests of fear such as fire, water, electricity, and heights as well as physical strength tests. The kicker is, this is a team event. That means not only do you have to complete each obstacle, but you must also help your teammates overcome their fears and physical abilities. My oldest brother Chris participated in one a couple of years ago, and said it was one of the most intense, crazy, and fun things he's ever done. I'm still questioning whether or not he took one of those electrical shocks to the dome because it doesn't sound like fun.

In life, there are constant obstacles in our way that are trying to keep us from knowing our position in Christ as sons and daughters. These obstacles keep us in bondage to sin and when we live in the 'to do' list mentality of Christianity, it keeps us from actually enjoying God. In this chapter, we are going to look at several of these obstacles in a practical way. My hope is that many of us will be set free from the chains that keep us from enjoying the grace we receive from our loving Father.

UNBELIEF – we have a belief problem, not a sin problem

The Scriptures are clear that one must believe Jesus to be the Savior of the world and accept the gift of grace He offers. Many people can get there. They can receive Jesus and begin a relationship with Him, but what most people have a problem with, is actually believing they are made righteous through this belief in Jesus. Abraham believed and it was credited to him as righteousness (Romans 4:3). So then, how do we become righteous? By believing God to be who He says He is! Yet, we refuse to believe God is love. We tend to easily forget that He's gracious, patient, and kind. We ignore that He genuinely cares about the major and minor details of our lives. Therefore, we refuse to believe God when He calls us His sons and daughters. We think our behavior determines our stance before Him. Friends, the problem of sin has already been paid for in full on the cross. We think there is no way God can love us as we are and that is a tragedy in and of itself.

I heard my pastor, Channock Banet, say this for the first time when he preached a sermon around the idea, "we don't have a sin problem - we have a belief problem." This is very important for us to grasp because the battle is no longer with sin; the battle lies between our ears…the battle is about what we believe, or in this case, Who we believe. As we talked about in Chapter 6, it never made sense to me when people told me the Spirit was convicting me of past sin. Why would the Spirit convict me of something that has already been paid for on the cross? The Spirit's job is not to convict me, but to convince me that living for Jesus is better than any sin I could find myself indulged in. Rick Warren says, "Behind every sin you commit is a lie you've believed."[1] When I sin, it's because of a lie I have believed about that sin. The lie that I need it, when I don't. The lie that it will help or change my life when the only person that can help and change my life is Jesus. Sin is not the issue anymore. It was crucified along with Jesus. As I heard Apostle Tony Fitzgerald say, "Jesus doesn't even want your sins because the last time He took them, it killed Him!" We are forgiven, permanently!

However, it seems like Christians love to talk about sin more than who Jesus really is. What would our lives look like if we realized our sins don't separate us from God? Because if our sins separated us from God, we would all be screwed. The only thing that separates us from God is not believing in His Son Jesus. This is also why we can live for Jesus and still fall short sometimes. What we don't teach very well is that the simplicity of Christianity is all about reminding ourselves that God loves us and calls us His children. It is this grace that enables us to defeat temptations when they come. It's time for us to truly believe God to be who He says He is. It's time for us to truly believe that God loves us, accepts us, and values us.

GUILT, SHAME & CONDEMNATION – Satan's oldest tricks in the book

One of the biggest ways Satan attacks believers today is through guilt, shame and condemnation. He constantly likes to talk about and bring things up from the past. The Christian cliché response to this is, "When Satan brings up your past, remind him of his future." It's corny but so true! Our past has no power, nor does it affect the way God feels about us. There is a reason why Scripture addresses this in both Romans 8:1 and John 3:17-18. There is now no condemnation for those who believe! Satan will try to condemn us but we cannot listen to those lies. He knows that if he can distract us from the truth of our position before God, we will constantly feel unworthy to follow God. But Jesus dealt with our sin on the cross so we could be worthy, righteous, and loved by God simply by our belief. Jesus never used guilt, shame, or condemnation to lead people to God. Once we use any of those three to motivate or scare people into a relationship with God, salvation becomes works based instead of gospel based. When we talk about Jesus, do we move people through shame or grace? It's time for us to rise up and start walking like sons and daughters because God wants to shine His love in and through us.

OUR THOUGHTS – The way we think determines the way we live

In the movie *American Sniper*, there is a scene where Chris Kyle is talking to fellow Navy SEAL Marc Lee that magnifies the reality of what we filter through our minds. As a sniper, Chris wanted to leave his position to help on the ground...

> Chris Kyle: "I'll tell you something. If these Marines keep rushing in like they're doing, they're going to get their asses shot off."
>
> Marc Lee: "Well, they're Marines. They don't get the training we do. Half these guys were civilians six months ago."
>
> Chris Kyle: "Well, let's coach 'em up. I'll show them how team guys do it. I'll lead the unit on the street."
>
> Marc Lee: "No, I can't do that. We need you on over watch."
>
> Chis Kyle: "Come on, if I'm on the street, Marc..."
>
> Marc Lee: "House to house is the deadliest job here, man. You got some sort of savior complex?"
>
> Chris Kyle: "I just want to get the bad guys but if I can't see them, I can't shoot them."
>
> Marc Lee: "Look, all these guys, they know your name. They feel invincible with you up there."
>
> Chris Kyle: "They're not."
>
> Marc Lee: "They are if they think they are."

Those marines knew the greatest sniper in the world was on his post watching over them. And when the greatest sniper in the world is on your team watching over you, there is a confidence resting in your soul. A confidence that enables you to be bold, diligent, and unstoppable. Because they believed they were invincible, they were.

Why do many believers tend to forget how big and strong God is but are quick to talk about the sometimes-overwhelming attacks of Satan? We have the greatest power in the world not only walking with us through every season but IN us in every season. Isaiah 54:17 tells us, "There is no weapon formed against us that will prosper." Notice however, that it doesn't say there will be no weapons against us. There will definitely be weapons against us, that's a promise! But these weapons won't prevail or prosper! We have the same power that raised Jesus from the grave living inside us. We are victorious because Jesus is victorious! What would our world look like if we lived like victors instead of victims?

This is why the thoughts we allow to gain ground in our minds are important. The Bible constantly talks about filtering our thoughts and knowing our position as children of God. Romans 12:2 says to be transformed by the renewing of our minds. Transforming is like weeding. It's a process that no one likes but is very necessary in order to see healthy things grow. Weeds grow because nothing is being done. We need to groom (transform) our gardens (minds). So how do we transform our minds? By constantly reminding ourselves of who our daddy is! By dwelling on His great love! By focusing on the reality that He calls us His sons and daughters. By fixing our eyes on Jesus.

2 Corinthians 10:5 says to take captive every thought and make it obedient to Christ. To take captive is a serious phrase. It implies we won't be able to control all the thoughts we have, but that we do have the power to control the thoughts we hold on to. We must capture wrong thoughts

and send them back to hell because that's where they came from. Our minds are either engaged by the father of lies or the Father of Love. The one we listen to will change our attitude, determine our direction, and influence our affections. Carlos Rodriguez says, "The father of lies has no intention of pushing our hand to do the wrong thing. His strategy is to convince us of our wrong value, for sinning is natural if we believe we are sinners as sonship will be natural when we believe we are God's sons!"[2]

The power we have over our thought life is incredible because we have the ability to overcome our circumstantial facts by trusting God. It's not about gaining new conditions or changing the surroundings; rather, it's about new thoughts and perspectives in the midst of the same conditions and same surroundings. As Rodriquez says, "While God speaks to our hearts day by day, the enemy speaks lies to our minds constantly. And the way we manage our daily thoughts, determines which father we get our identity from."[3] It's time to take back our minds and allow them to be saturated in the truth of who we are – sons and daughters of the most high King!

COMPARISON – Do we know how happy we would be if we didn't have information about our friends and family to compare life with?

We play this game called comparison all day long. The Bible wouldn't advise us to not compare if we all didn't do it one way or another. We see evil on the news and think we're better than the person committing crimes. Then we see great things people are doing in our society and think we're worse off because we're not doing anything. So starts this endless cycle of thinking we're better or worse than the people around us. We create this scale, measuring a person's worth based on their performance and then tend to believe God judges us by this same scale. And all of this starts with the seed called 'comparison'.

During my time at Elevation Church, I heard Pastor Steven Furtick say this phrase maybe a hundred times. He would tell the church and the staff, "Quit comparing your behind the scenes work with everyone else's highlight reels." How true! It's almost comical how often I find myself comparing my life to others. In other words, I'll compare my Chapter 5 of life with other people's Chapter 25. Then I'll get ticked that I don't see the results I feel I deserve but only because so and so got results this year and I didn't. Comparison only robs me of staying content and rips the blessings right up from underneath me. Let's face it – we all love to see the highlights. There is a reason why ESPN only shows the buzzer beaters, OT winners, grand slams, and 80-yard touchdown passes. ESPN doesn't highlight the process of the offseason to mini-camp, then to training camp. They don't show the grueling practices or the broken bones and rehab. They don't show the workouts or the blood, sweat, and tears. We only see the glory! Rarely do we see the process of what it took to get the glory. In the ministry world, we do this all time. We see the church attendance, finances, and spiritual growth, and we wish our behind the scenes work would be noticed like the highlights of whatever church we compare ourselves to. We do this with our families, our jobs, vacations, and materialistic possessions. And if we aren't careful, we'll even do this with our own personal walk with Jesus. We are never more like Satan than when we compare.

One thing we need to realize that will help us kill this

comparison thing is understanding that being blessed is a mindset. We can believe the lie that people are blessed based on their behavior OR we can know we're blessed because we're sons and daughters of the King. According to Ephesians 1:3 we are already blessed with every spiritual blessing. We are blessed not by receiving more perishable stuff but by knowing that Father God calls us by name. I wonder how many blessings we miss because we're too busy wishing we had what our neighbors have. Again, what we focus our attention on will determine our direction and influence our affections. It will ultimately affect the way we love people!

GOOD WORKS – We don't go to heaven because we're 'good'

We are not saved by our works. We are saved by believing Jesus to be the Son of God. My behavior does not determine my position in heaven. My behavior determines how much of heaven flows through me to others while I'm still here on Earth. Unfortunately, we are often taught to be 'good' people. Jesus isn't interested in behavior modification. He's interested in us! Again, we are not saved BY works. However, we are saved FOR works. When we begin to understand grace, our lives won't contradict it. We will begin to see God's love flowing through us to everyone we meet because we are so captivated by a God who is so captivated by us.

Understanding this takes off the pressure to perform. When we're trying to do good things to earn love from God without realizing He already loves us, our motives become exposed. Genuine love flows from a position of sonship, a position not based on behavior. Many of us strive on Earth to one day hear our Father in Heaven say, "Well done, good and faithful servant." But again, understanding our position as sons and daughters brings this passage to light. I first heard this thought from my friend Reggi Beasley when he preached on the parable of the talents from Matthew 25. This parable is not about what they did but rather about whom they believed. It's a parable about advancing the Kingdom of God and not living in fear – doing works not to gain a position but from a position they already had. A position as children in the Kingdom of God. We tend to believe this passage is speaking of when we get to Heaven. We hope God will look at us and say, "Well done my good and faithful servant," based on what we did on Earth (behavior). However, that is not what is going on here. In fact, that sentence is not going to be said based on what we did. That sentence is going to be said based on whether or not we believed and trusted in Jesus. Reggi said it this way, "There is only ONE good and faithful servant to have ever lived, and His name is Jesus." So the question is, do we believe Jesus to be the Savior of the world? If so, we will be credited as a good and faithful servant on Jesus' behalf! So please stop striving to become a good and faithful servant and start realizing you already are a good and faithful servant because the good and faithful servant lives in you. Your behavior is a by-product of truly knowing your position as a son or daughter.

OLD COVENANT LAW – We don't live under the Law of Moses

This is probably the biggest obstacle to grace that most people are not aware of. There are tons of other books that do a much better job explaining old covenant law vs. new covenant grace. Therefore, I'm just going to briefly explain this. The old covenant law represents the Law of Moses, or better known as the 10 commandments. On top of the 10 commandments were 603 commands that Jews were supposed to follow in order to be "holy". That totals 613 laws/commands or 248 things one must do (plus) 365 things one must not do (equals) 613. That is a lot of commands!! Some of these commands were ridiculous, like you couldn't wear more than one kind of fabric (so if your shirt is made of cotton and polyester you were breaking the law). Some of these commands, we would all agree, are good. For example, do not murder or do not boil a young goat in its mother's milk, since it is a ritual of those who worship false gods (Exodus 23:19). Yeah, that was a real thing.

The sad reality of these laws is the fact that God didn't want them in the first place (refer to Chapter 7). God didn't want Israel to have to go through a priest in order to have fellowship with Him because God has always wanted a personal and direct relationship with us. Today, we live under the new covenant or the covenant of love and grace, not a covenant of rules! We don't live under the 10 commandments (although they are good things). The only purpose of the 10 commandments is to point us to Jesus. That is why people use them in evangelism. All the 10 commandments do is show us that everyone is guilty and in need of a Savior. Even the 10 commandments themselves show us the picture of grace. The first five deal with our relationship with God. The last five deal with our relationship with man. Five is the number for grace. We are to relate to God in accepting His grace. We are to relate to man with giving grace. The law only has the power to reveal sin, it does not have the power to remove it. Welcome Jesus' sacrifice. We are to look at the old covenant law and worship Jesus because He fulfilled all the laws on our behalf.

The religious leaders and Pharisees were more focused on the traditions of their religious duties rather than resting in the peace and hope of God's unconditional love. Sounds like a lot of us today. We like to criticize celebrities and judge those who do not live with the same convictions or beliefs as us. Especially for believers, as long as others seem worse than us, we feel pretty good about ourselves. This was the exact mentality of the Pharisees. Here's a challenging question: did you know that anyone can have the spirit of a Pharisee in any given moment of any given day? The problem of the Pharisees wasn't the law they were striving to obey, but rather the lack of grace they offered to those who broke it. Jesus consistently challenged the Pharisees and was angry with them not because of their laws, but because they hurt people in the name of religion! Gregory Boyd says, "It is important for us to notice that religious sin is the only sin Jesus publically confronted...Religious sin is unique in that it is the only sin that can keep a community from fulfilling the commission to unconditionally love and embrace everyone."[4] This is why Jesus' message was so offensive to the Jewish leaders, because He audaciously accepted and loved everyone! As Brady Boyd puts it, "During his earthly ministry, every time Jesus asked a crowd how they were doing, the Pharisees among them responded by rattling off a report card...If we're not careful, as soon as we experience victory over a particular habit or sin in our lives, we might become wildly intolerant of that propensity in others."[5] Whenever we do not love and offer grace to others, we're acting like a Pharisee. This is a constant reminder for me to love and give grace to the people

I tend to dislike the most. Even Apostle Peter had to be reminded of grace in Galatians 2. So the question remains: how do we kill the Pharisee in our own lives? By introducing him to grace. By injecting Him with Jesus! Galatians 2:20 says, "It is no longer I who lives, but Christ who lives in me!"

Jesus did not die to promote a moral code of conduct. He died to prove to us how much He loves us. He died not only to conquer sin but also to destroy death so we might have life and life to the fullest. The 'law' we live by today is love (John 13:34). Following Jesus is way more simple than we make it. Yes, it is difficult in different seasons but Jesus is the only One that can bring us peace in those difficult seasons. The people that have the hardest time understanding grace and the new covenant are those that want to argue about having the old covenant still involved in our lives today. Here is the bottom line when living under the only 'law' we are to live by today – that being love. When we are truly being refined by God's love day by day, we won't put false gods before Jesus, we won't make idols, we'll honor our parents, and we won't murder, etc. When we truly start to live by love and stop holding rules over people's heads, lives will begin to actually change and the Kingdom of God continues to expand. Let's hold off on our judgments because that never encouraged anyone to follow Jesus. Rather, let's love people – even those we disagree with because that is what will truly change the world.

TOO GOOD TO BE TRUE – It really is the good news

The Gospel literally means the good news. Therefore, anything preached that is not good news is not the Gospel. Some people have a really hard time with grace being this amazing but that's why it's called *Amazing Grace*. Grace is even better than we think it is. The biggest tragedies in our world today are people who think it's too good to be true and simply deny it. Another tragedy occurs when we think we fully grasp or understand this person called Jesus. Walking with Jesus keeps getting better day after day and I find myself falling more in love with Him after dwelling on His grace.

Another obstacle to receiving this too good to be true news is preconceived knowledge of grace, because we think we've heard it before. Or worse, calling it "greasy grace", because we think we fully understand it and claim that it gives people an excuse to live like an idiot. Reality check: we don't need grace as an excuse to live like an idiot, that comes naturally. The same grace that saved us when we gave our life to Jesus is the same grace we need every day to sustain us. The Christian life begins with grace, continues with grace, and finishes with grace. We rely on the work of Christ for salvation, but the problem occurs when we think we need to work to keep it. The only work we need to do is continue to rest in the finished work of Jesus. His grace really is sufficient, the gospel really is good news, and Satan really does not want us to realize it.

WE FORGET TO PLAY – Christians are not called to be boring

I get so sad when people think Christians are boring. The problem however, isn't that they think that. The problem is many of us believers give them serious reasons to believe that. I was recently eating lunch at the local middle school with several of my middle school students. We were cracking jokes and having a great time. You can easily make an entire lunchroom laugh by making fart noises with your mouth. I know – it's why I work with students. Or maybe it's because adults are too up tight? ... Anyways, one of the students looked at me with a huge smile and said, "I can't believe you're a pastor, you're actually funny." At first I laughed with him but the longer I thought about it the more it rattled me. Why do people have this perception that Christians aren't funny, let alone fun? Christians should be full of life, living the most fun, abundant, and meaningful lives that life has to offer. I mean for real, we have the Lord of lords and King of kings living inside of us! We are not called to be boring. Go out and do something amazing and inspire someone. Go out and do something you're good at. Go out and do something adventurous! We have become so task oriented as a society that we have forgotten to play; we have forgotten to enjoy life and the people around us.

Why is it that we allow culture to tell us what fun is? Culture tells us to go get drunk at parties and sleep with as many people as possible. Culture tells us that debt is okay and we should buy things on impulse because we want it or feel like we deserve it. Culture tells us to look out for ourselves and do whatever it takes to make it to the top, even at the cost of our integrity and relationships. Culture tells us that porn is helpful for marriage or that divorce is an option if things don't work out as planned. Culture tells us that beauty is purchased and our image should be compared to photoshopped pictures on the cover of magazines. But all these lies we believe from culture only breed heartbreak, frustration, greed, confusion, and bitterness. Waking up in a bed next to someone you don't know is not fun. It's empty and awkward, and only produces shame and resentment. We need to stop allowing culture to define us and tell us how to have fun. I believe Christians should be the most fun, passionate, and creative people in the world since we have the Creator of the Universe living inside us! People should want us around because they know they'll be encouraged and better off from the time they spend with us. Our children shouldn't need a reason to 'rebel' because the Christian life should be the best life there is. It should be modeled in a way that produces fun, joyful, and alive people living life to the fullest and making a difference in our communities. We need to stop blaming culture and start changing it ourselves because at the end of the day…we are the culture.

CHAPTER 11

HEROES FOR SALE

This chapter is titled after one of my favorite hip-hop albums of all time. *Heroes For Sale*, released in 2013, by Andy Mineo. I cannot express to you in words how much I love hip-hop music. The moment the beat hits my ears, it's over. If you're lucky, you may get to experience my ridiculous dance moves. Let's just say I may be the only person who thinks I'm a good dancer!

Growing up, I listened to all kinds of artists. But the artists who resonated with me the most were the ones that talked about their real life experiences. Anyone can talk about sex, money, drugs, and power, but there are few who can engage a crowd with authentic lyrics, creative word play, flow, and heart pumping beats. There are even fewer who can make a difference through lyrics without being corny or weird. Enter Andy Mineo. I've been following this guy's music from the beginning. He not only possesses the four key ingredients to hip-hop, but I've seen his lyrics make a difference in the lives of people. I remember seeing him in concert during his *Heroes For Sale* release tour and he went into detail about the inspiration behind the name of his album. He explained the reality of not just American Christians, but Americans in general, when he talked about the fact that we all like to put our best foot forward. We all are guilty of selling the hero version of ourselves in an effort to gain acceptance, approval, love, and worth. It's why we look our best on our first date. It's why we put only positive things down on job resumes. It's why we walk into church acting like our families are perfect. It's why some don't even walk into church because they know everyone's wearing a mask. And it's this reason, why marriages are falling apart, drugs are around our students, and people are running to everything the world has to offer instead of running to an intimate and personal God. We offer hero versions of ourselves to others because we are scared that if we don't, people will see us for who we really are. It's time we put this hero version of ourselves up for sale because that's not who God intended us to be!

Removing this mask is hard because we believe the lie that we need it. However, when we wear a mask, it not only prevents us from showing our true colors but it also keeps us from seeing God for who He truly is: A loving God who accepts all our mess and loves us anyway! It's a slap in God's face to think He doesn't love us for who we really are. When we fake to be someone we're not, we in essence are saying God only loves the person we pretend to be. News flash: God knows we're a mess. He knows all the details of our lives. He knows our lies, schemes, and thoughts. He knows about every skeleton in our closet and even the ones we have forgotten about. But here's the best part – He loves us anyway. This is why His grace truly is amazing! His grace allows us to be open and honest. His grace empowers us to do the right things in life. His grace is a 'high' that is more freeing than any drug we could take. It's time to remove the mask and stop pretending to be someone we're not because God cannot bless the person we pretend to be. He wants to bless us, as we are, and show us that the real hero in life is Jesus. Once the mask is removed, He opens us up to His incredible love... a love that removes all shame, condemnation, and guilt; a love that will change us from the inside out.

Selling the hero version of ourselves and removing this mask is essential to living in freedom with Christ. These masks can look different for every person, but one mask that keeps us from living in sonship the most is the mask of the old covenant law. Thinking that our good deeds meet God's "requirements" actually causes more harm than good.

> We are not like Moses who would put a veil over his face to prevent the Israelites from seeing the end of what was passing away. But their minds were made dull, for to this day the same veil remains when the old covenant is read. It has not been removed, because only in Christ is it taken away. Even to this day when Moses is read, a veil covers their hearts. But whenever anyone turns to the Lord, the veil is taken away. Now the Lord is the Spirit, and where the Spirit of the Lord is, there is freedom.
> 2 Corinthians 3:13-17

We've talked about this all throughout this book that it's

not about keeping the law or the 613 commands of the old covenant. It's about simply believing God to be who He says He is, believing in our sonship and daughterhood, and loving like we have been loved by Christ. No more law, just grace. This is what takes away the chains of bondage. This is where the Spirit of the Lord is, which brings freedom like nothing else. When we try to do life with a checklist of good deeds, we remain dull or exhausted. Only when we focus on the love and grace of Jesus Christ are we enabled to remove the masks in our lives and stand accepted and approved before God. We must take off the mask of good deeds and fronting like we're a good believer because it's tiring trying to be someone we're not. Masks cover up needs, and Jesus can't meet our needs until we give Him our mess. It's heartbreaking to watch as some people would rather be miserable with their masks than free with Jesus. It's time to let go of who we think we want to be and start walking in the freedom of Christ!

You might be sitting there thinking to yourself, wow this kind of love sounds amazing. But your hesitation lies in the fine print. The reason why many people wear masks is because this grace and love from God is not offered in the churches they attend or the Christians they know. The thing that bothers me the most about some church goers is probably the thing that bothers you the most if you're still a skeptic about Jesus. It's that thing that causes distance that Satan loves to use in American churches today. That thing known as judgment. Judgment happens because people don't understand that grace has nothing to do with rules and labels. What legalists and judgmental Christians do is they focus on the outside. They say things like, 'if you don't do this or do that, then you're not saved'. They focus on skin color, smell, clothes, tattoos or piercings, actions, and any other thing they can look down on others for in an attempt to raise themselves up. They claim Christ, but that is not the Gospel, nor does it represent Jesus very well at all.

If God's love and grace are unconditional, why do we as humans put conditions on them? That's a question you might want to read again. Before I go on, I want to apologize to anyone who has been hurt by me or any other Bible believing Christian due to judgment. Regardless of what believers of Jesus act like, there is no judgmental attitude coming from God. God does not judge from outward appearances. He doesn't care what you look like or where you've been. He cares about you, as you are, right now. He wants you! Unconditional love means we have absolutely nothing to prove! So stop trying so hard and start trusting in His unadulterated love!

True love from a good Father is amazing. That is who God is! But love is not just something we can think about; it's something we can see. Love is an action and it must be proven one way or another. The greatest act of love can be found when Jesus died for us all. John 15:13 says, "Greater love has no one than this: to lay down one's life for one's friends." 1 John 3:16 says, "This is how we know what love is: Jesus Christ laid down his life for us. And we ought to lay down our lives for our brothers and sisters." Jesus paid the ultimate price to reverse what happened in the garden. But if you're anything like me, you grew up with the question: God, why even put a tree in the garden that could cause death? The simple answer is, there had to be a tree because love is only proven when you have options. Love is proven not just in what you say 'yes' to, but also in what you say 'no' to. When I said, 'I Do' to my wife, I also said, 'I Don't' to every other girl in the world! Johnnie Moore says, "God could not design a man who could choose to love him without giving man the freedom not to."[1] This is why God does not force us into a relationship with Him nor is He controlling us like a puppet master. He gives us the choice to choose Him and even if we deny Him, He is still crazy about us (Romans 5:8).

We think sin in Genesis 3 is what Jesus came to conquer but sin is never mentioned in Genesis 3. Yes, the concept of sin is all throughout this passage but what is mentioned is separation from God, or death, or the tree of the knowledge of good and evil. This tree is so important to understand because we tend to focus on the evil part and not on the good part. The tree is called, 'the knowledge of good and evil'. So guess what causes death? Knowledge without God. That means knowledge that is both good and evil, apart from God, is what causes death. The problem with the Christian life occurs when we try to be good in our own efforts. Proverbs 14:12 says, "There is a way that appears to be right, but in the end it leads to death." Without resting in the finished work of Jesus, we will run ourselves dry trying to earn our place in the Kingdom of God. Knowledge that is good without God leads us to believe the Gospel is about behavior modification when it's not.

Let's break this tree down even further. The knowledge of evil is what makes us aware of our issues, but the knowledge of good is what makes us try to fix those issues without God. This happened immediately after Adam and Eve ate of the fruit. When they realized they were naked, they grabbed fig leaves as if fig leaves were going to fix their nudity. I find it humorous they used fig leaves because fig leaves will not get the job done in terms of trying to cover up the goods. However, it was God who killed the first animal and clothed them with garments of skin in Genesis 3:21. God took away their shame and nudity with the shedding of blood in the garden just like He takes away our shame and nudity with the shedding of His Son's blood on the cross.

Here's the big issue with the tree of the knowledge of good and evil. The knowledge of good has done more to separate the church today than the knowledge of evil. We tend to call Christianity – good behavior, but notice that the branches of the knowledge of good are in the same tree as the branches of the knowledge of evil. Our knowledge of good is our answer to the knowledge of evil; and if we think our behavior is what makes God happy then we have missed the point of the Gospel. Even Judas hangs himself on the tree of the knowledge of good and evil apart from grace because he couldn't find forgiveness for himself. Living for Jesus is not about making rules in our lives. It's not even about making us behave better. It's about being filled with LIFE in Christ. It's about being aware of the constant presence of God in our lives. It's about falling in love with a God that is so in love with us!

Jesus died for our good and evil works and He wants us to trust Him and rest in His finished work on the cross. The things Jesus came to conquer were sin and death so we could have LIFE. Let's not get so caught up in rules and sin that we don't even realize the LIFE we are missing out on.

Here it is in a nutshell: Just as one person did it wrong and got us in all this trouble with sin and death, another person did it right and got us out of it. But more than just getting us out of trouble, he got us into life! One man said no to God and put many people in the wrong; one man said yes to God and put many in the right. All that passing laws against sin

did was produce more lawbreakers. But sin didn't, and doesn't, have a chance in competition with the aggressive forgiveness we call *grace*. When it's sin versus grace, grace wins hands down. All sin can do is threaten us with death, and that's the end of it. Grace, because God is putting everything together again through the Messiah, invites us into life—a life that goes on and on and on, world without end.
Romans 5:18-21 The Message.

Jesus is our hero. Not because He comes and destroys our enemies but because He shed His blood on the cross for His enemies. He's the One who has rescued us from sin and death. He is our lover and friend, ascribing to us unsurpassable worth. The cross is not the symbol of Christianity, the empty tomb is! Jesus is alive and He's freeing us from the religious grave clothes that keep us in bondage. It's time to break free from rituals and rules and run into the loving embrace of the Father - because *we are His beloved!*

A PERSONAL THANKS TO...

My wife – You inspire me! I love you to Ukraine and back.

Mom – I love you. Thank you for your endless support and encouragement. You are an incredible woman of God.

Dad – Thank you for being you. Your leadership and integrity are second to none. I love you.

Chris – Thank you for helping with the editing process. I'm very grateful for you and our friendship.

Brett – Thank you for always encouraging me with your support. I appreciate it more than you know.

Connor – Thank you for not killing me. I'm proud of the man you are becoming.

The Martin family – Thank you for welcoming me into the family as your own. I'm thankful for all of you!

Channock Banet & Reggi Beasley – Your friendship means the world to me. Thank you for making me better and being two of the best friends anyone could ask for.

Bishop Jamie Englehart & Bishop Dan Dyer – Thank you for your guidance and influence. I appreciate the time you take to pour into our team!

Pastor Daryl & Linda Banet – Thank you for being obedient and starting Cornerstone Church. We love you!

Louise Stumler – God knows we couldn't do anything without you. Thank you for being our resident superwoman.

Aleshia Shouse – Thank you for helping edit and for being a rockstar. You made this process so much easier!

David Semenyna – Thank you for challenging me to get this thing done. You're an incredible friend.

Jack Janigian, Josh Lindstrom, Dan Plantz, Kevin Stacker – I am who I am because of the influence of you four. Thank you for shaping me into the man I am today.

Dr. David Wheeler – Thank you for mentoring me during my college years. I appreciate you.

Jay Rabon – Words can't express how large of an impact you made on my life during my time at Elevation. I hope to be as good of a husband and father as you are!

Apostle Tony Fitzgerald – This book became what it is when I heard you say, "The richest places in the world are graveyards, because that's where dreams, songs, and books that weren't written have died." Thank you!

NOTES

Introduction
[1] Timm, Eric Samuel. *Static Jedi*. Lake Mary, FL: Charisma House, 2013. Print.

Chapter 1 – Prove It
[1] Michigan Memories by Paul Braun, 2008.
http://www.uwathletics.com/blogs/default.aspx?postid=168
1

Chapter 2 - Stauros
[1] http://www.4truth.net/world-religions/islam/
[2]
http://www.4truth.net/fourtruthpbworld.aspx?pageid=8589
952127
[3]
http://www.4truth.net/fourtruthpbworld.aspx?pageid=8589
952141

Chapter 3 – Who's Your Daddy?
[1] Email from Channock Banet, July 10, 2015.
[2]
http://taylorandsarahbrooks.blogspot.com/2013/04/parents
-word-about-Instagram.html?m=1
[3] Brennan Manning sermon, "God loves you as you are, not as you should be."
[4] Ibid.

Chapter 4 – Let's Get Naked
[1] Frost, Jack. *Spiritual Slavery to Spiritual Sonship*. Shippensburg, PA: Destiny Image, 2006. 23.
[2] Hiles, Lynn. *The Revelation of Jesus Christ: An Open Letter to the Church from a Modern Perspective of the Book of Revelation.* Shippensburg, PA: Destiny Image, 2007. Print. 45.

[3] Hiles, Lynn, Dr. *Unforced Rhythms of Grace*. Great Cacapon, WV: Lynn Hiles Ministries, 2011. Print. 6-7.

Chapter 5 – Slaying Santa
[1] Boyd, Gregory A. *Repenting of Religion: Turning from Judgment to the Love of God*. Grand Rapids, MI: Baker, 2004. Print. 59.
[2] Farley, Andrew. *The Naked Gospel: The Truth You May Never Hear in Church*. Grand Rapids, MI: Zondervan, 2009. Print. 191.
[3] Ibid. 168.
[4] Ibid. 169.

Chapter 6 – Like An Angel
[1] Twitter. Lecrae tweeted this on May 24, 2012.
[2] Moore, Johnnie. *What Am I Supposed to Do with My Life?: God's Will Demystified*. N.p.: n.p., n.d. Print. 49.
[3] Greear, J. D. *Gospel*. Nashville, TN: B & H Pub. Group, 2011. Print. 51.
[4] Frost, Jack. *Spiritual Slavery to Spiritual Sonship*. Shippensburg, PA: Destiny Image, 2006. Print. 65.

Chapter 7 – Grace Changes Everything
[1] Greear, J. D. *Gospel*. Nashville, TN: B & H Pub. Group, 2011. Print. 100.
[2] Farley, Andrew. *God without Religion: Can It Really Be This Simple?* Grand Rapids, MI: Baker, 2011. Print. 261.

Chapter 8 – Weapons Of Mass Distraction
[1] Ramsey, Dave. *The Total Money Makeover: A Proven Plan for Financial Fitness*. Nashville: Thomas Nelson Pub., 2003. Print.
[2] Twitter. Tullian Tchividjian tweeted this on February 15, 2013.
[3] Keller, Timothy. *The Reason for God: Belief in an Age of Skepticism*. New York: Dutton, 2008. Print. 30.
[4] Boyd, Brady. *Sons and Daughters: Spiritual Orphans Finding Our Way Home*. Grand Rapids, MI: Zondervan, 2012. Print. 175.

[5] Timm, Eric Samuel. *Static Jedi*. N.p.: n.p., n.d. Print. 60-61.
[6] Twitter. Wigglesworth Quotes tweeted this on May 14, 2014.

Chapter 9 - Cannibalism
[1] Boyd, Gregory A. *Repenting of Religion: Turning from Judgment to the Love of God*. Grand Rapids, MI: Baker, 2004. Print. 102-103.
[2] Ibid. 60. 187.
[3] Boyd, Brady. *Sons and Daughters: Spiritual Orphans Finding Our Way Home*. Grand Rapids, MI: Zondervan, 2012. Print. 46.
[4] http://www.christianitytoday.com/le/2012/december-online-only/going-to-hell-with-ted-haggard.html?start=1

Chapter 10 – Tough Mudder
[1] Facebook. Rick Warren posted this on June 22, 2011.
[2] Rodriguez, Carlos A. *Designed for Inheritance: A Discovery of Sonship*. Toronto, ON, Canada: Catch The Fire Books, 2014. Print. 76.
[3] Ibid. 77.
[4] Boyd, Gregory A. *Repenting of Religion: Turning from Judgment to the Love of God*. Grand Rapids, MI: Baker, 2004. Print. 203-204.
[5] Boyd, Brady. *Sons and Daughters: Spiritual Orphans Finding Our Way Home*. Grand Rapids, MI: Zondervan, 2012. Print. 48, 45.

Chapter 11 – Heroes For Sale
[1] Moore, Johnnie. *Honestly: Really Living What We Say We Believe*. Eugene, Or.: Harvest House, 2011. Print. 121.